Doing Business:

An Independent Evaluation

Taking the Measure of the World Bank-IFC
Doing Business Indicators

165101

2008
The World Bank
Washington, D.C.

World Bank InfoShop
E-mail: pic@worldbank.org
Telephone: 202-458-5454
Facsimile: 202-522-1500

Independent Evaluation Group
Knowledge Programs and Evaluation Capacity
Development (IEGKE)
E-mail: eline@worldbank.org
Telephone: 202-458-4497
Facsimile: 202-522-3125

 Printed on Recycled Paper

Contents

Abbreviations

AAA	Analytical and advisory activities
BEE	Business Enabling Environment
CAE	Country Assistance Evaluation
CAS	Country Assistance Strategy
CPIA	Country Policy and Institutional Assessment
CPS	Country Partnership Strategy
DB	Doing Business
DFID	Department for International Development (United Kingdom)
EODB	Ease of doing business
ESW	Economic and sector work
FDI	Foreign direct investment
FIAS	Foreign Investment Advisory Service
FPD	Financial and private sector development
GDP	Gross domestic product
GNI	Gross national income
ICA	Investment Climate Assessment
ICR	Implementation Completion Report
IDA	International Development Association
IEG	Independent Evaluation Group
IFC	International Finance Corporation
ILO	International Labour Organization
MCC	Millennium Challenge Corporation (U.S.)
MIGA	Multilateral Investment Guarantee Agency
NGO	Nongovernmental organization
OECD	Organisation for Economic Co-operation and Development
OHADA	L'Organisation pour l'Harmonisation en Afrique du Droit des Affaires/Organization for the Harmonization of Business Law in Africa
PEP	Private enterprise partnership
PSD	Private sector development
PwC	PricewaterhouseCoopers
TA	Technical assistance
USAID	United States Agency for International Development
VAT	Value added tax
WBG	World Bank Group
WDI	World Development Indicators
WDR	*World Development Report*

Glossary and Conventions Used in this Report

DB 2007 data	The data gathered during 2006 and published in late 2006 in the report entitled *Doing Business 2007*
DB 2007 revised	The data set posted on the DB Web site replacing the DB 2007 data as originally published
DB 2008 data	The data gathered during 2007 and published in October 2007 in the report entitled *Doing Business 2008*
Index	A type of subindicator composed of several binary criteria (such as the *difficulty of firing* index)
Indicator	One of the 10 main DB indicators (for example, *starting a business*)
Ranking	The ordinal ranking of a country
Rating	The cardinal number or index score of a country on a particular indicator (such as 16 procedures or 430 days)
Subindicator	One of the 32 elements comprising the 10 indicators (for example, number of days to start a business, number of procedures to start a business) that go into the calculation of the *ease of doing business* aggregate ranking.

Acknowledgments

This evaluation was conducted by a team led by Deepa Chakrapani and Victoria Elliott. Shonar Lala led the evaluation in its initial stages. Other team members were Victoria Y. Chang, John Eriksson, Giancarlo Marchesi, and Stoyan Tenev. A background paper was prepared by Simon Commander (director, Center for New and Emerging Markets at the London Business School) with Katrin Tinn. Additional inputs were provided by James Heyes and Salvatore Spada. Marinella Yadao and Yezena Yimer provided administrative support. William Hurlbut and Caroline McEuen edited the report.

The peer reviewers for this report were: Lily Chu (World Bank), Neil Gregory (IFC), Stephen Golub (Swarthmore College), Vijaya Ramachandran (Center for Global Development and Georgetown University), and Guven Sak (TEPAV, Economic Policy Research Foundation of Turkey).

The evaluation team thanks its numerous interviewees among Bank Group staff, individuals in client countries, and Doing Business informants. It also appreciates the cooperation it received from the Doing Business team.

Director-General, Evaluation: *Vinod Thomas*
Director, Independent Evaluation Group–World Bank: *Cheryl Gray*
Group Manager, IEG Corporate and Global Evaluation and Methods: *Mark Sundberg*
Task Managers: *Victoria Elliott and Deepa Chakrapani*

Foreword

Institutions matter a great deal for development, and a country's regulatory institutions are vital for the pace and quality of economic growth. The Doing Business (DB) indicators deal with the part of the regulatory regime that governs the start-up, operation, and growth of businesses. Improvements in the climate for businesses can potentially generate jobs and incomes. DB is built on the premise that these firms are more likely to flourish if they have to abide by fewer, cheaper, and simpler regulations.

By ranking countries on selected dimensions of business regulation, the DB report has attracted considerable attention and has become one of the Bank Group's flagship knowledge products. And, like any rating exercise, it has also provoked important questions and concerns, both inside and outside of the Bank Group. This evaluation takes an independent look at the relevance, reliability, and usefulness of this innovative exercise.

DB assesses the burden of regulation on firms without aiming to capture the social or economy-wide benefits that regulations yield, such as safety, environmental protection, worker protection, or transparency. DB offers a consistent yardstick for comparing countries on regulation as seen from the firm's private point of view. But a complete appreciation of the quality of the business climate must also measure the quality of infrastructure, labor skills, competition policies, and other determinants and outcomes of investment and profitability.

DB has developed an impressive system for gathering standard information from lawyers and other informants in more than 170 countries. However, the number of informants on each topic and country is small, making it difficult to measure confidence levels around the country rankings. The evaluation recommends that DB recruit more, and more diverse, informants; disclose the number of informants; and be more transparent about changes in published data.

The evaluation found that DB has often sparked constructive debate among country authorities and business interests about ways of making regulation simpler and lighter on firms. Some fear that it can distort the policy priorities of authorities or the Bank Group by extending the encouragement for less regulatory burden, to the discouragement of good and valuable regulations. Even though this seems not to have happened, the context and perspective on what DB really measures or addresses are crucial for policy makers and practitioners to keep in mind.

In coming years, regulatory actions will become increasingly important as countries address challenges such as migration, health, and climate change. It will be crucial to emphasize both the need for efficiency in the implementation of a regulation and the benefits that a good regulation can bring. That is why it is important to discuss the usefulness of DB and how it can be improved, along with the context in which good regulations need to be implemented.

Vinod Thomas
Director-General, Evaluation

Village shop at dusk, lit by solar panels, Sri Lanka. Photo courtesy of Dominic Sansoni/World Bank.

Preface

Doing Business (DB), the annual World Bank-IFC benchmarking exercise launched in 2004, is one of the Bank Group's flagship knowledge products. It aims to measure the costs to firms of business regulations in 178 countries and ranks the countries along 10 dimensions. It also aims to advance the World Bank Group's private sector development agenda by motivating and informing the design of regulatory reforms, enriching international initiatives on development effectiveness, and informing theory. By ranking countries and spotlighting both leaders and laggards, DB has attracted the interest of senior policy makers and is claimed to have inspired reforms on business climate issues. DB's lively communications style has helped give the DB indicators an international profile.

DB has critics as well as fans. Some have questioned the reliability and objectivity of its measurements. Others doubt the relevance of the issues it addresses or fear it may unduly dominate countries' reform agendas at the expense of more crucial development objectives. And the attention given to the indicators may inadvertently signal that the World Bank Group values less burdensome business regulations more highly than its other strategies for poverty reduction and sustainable development.

This IEG evaluation of the DB indicators provides an independent view of DB's strengths and weaknesses, in response to interest expressed by members of the Board of Executive Directors of the World Bank Group and others. The evaluation assesses the methods and processes underlying the construction of the indicators; the relevance of the indicators to desired intermediate outcomes; and their use by World Bank Group staff, policy makers, and other relevant stakeholders. To the extent that countries may seek to implement efficient regulatory frameworks to guide other areas of development, such as health, environment, energy, and climate change, the Bank Group could use lessons from the DB initiative to help countries develop ways to benchmark the soundness of their regulatory framework and track improvements over time.

To carry out the evaluation, the IEG team commissioned a literature review, analyzed the ratings and underlying data published by DB, validated DB's methodology by interviewing a sample of their informants, and analyzed the DB indicators' relevance and use in 13 randomly selected countries by interviewing Bank and IFC staff, country officials, and experts. Appendix A explains the methodology in detail.

The report has five sections: chapter 1 reviews the intellectual underpinnings of the DB indicators. Chapter 2 reports on how DB collects and assembles data. Chapters 3 and 4 discuss the relevance of the dimensions measured by the exercise and their use inside and outside the Bank. Chapter 5 presents findings and recommendations.

Women sort roses for export to Europe at fair-trade company Kiliflora (Tanzania). Photo courtesy of Jorgen Schytte/Still Pictures.

Executive Summary

*D*oing Business (DB), an annual World Bank-IFC publication launched in 2004, is one of the Bank Group's flagship knowledge products. It measures the burden of selected business regulations in 178 countries and ranks the countries on 10 dimensions. The program's stated objective is to advance the World Bank Group's private sector development agenda in four ways: motivate reforms through country benchmarking; inform the design of reforms; enrich international initiatives on development effectiveness; and inform theory.

This independent evaluation of the DB indicators assesses the methods and processes underlying the construction of the indicators; the relevance of the indicators to desired intermediate outcomes; and their use by World Bank Group staff, policy makers, and other stakeholders. It finds that the indicators have been highly effective in drawing attention to the burdens of business regulation, but cannot by themselves capture other key dimensions of a country's business climate, the benefits of regulation, or key related aspects of development effectiveness. Thus, the Bank Group and stakeholders need to consider the DB indicators in a country context and interpret them accordingly.

The Underlying Framework of the DB Indicators

The DB exercise is anchored in research that links characteristics of a country's business environment to firm performance, and thence to macroeconomic outcomes. The regulatory framework—the part of the business environment that DB measures—has been shown to be associated with firm performance, but its association with macroeconomic outcomes is less clear. Many other factors affect macroeconomic outcomes, and the direction of causality between regulation and economic outcomes is very

difficult to isolate. Since regulations generate social benefits as well as private costs, what is good for an individual firm is not necessarily good for the economy or society as a whole. Therefore, policy implications are not always clear-cut, and the right level and type of regulation is a matter of policy choice in each country.

The DB exercise reflects the limitations inherent in the underlying research. As an exercise in cross-country comparison, DB is not intended to, and cannot, capture country nuances. Firms' investment decisions also depend on variables not measured by the DB indicators, such as the cost and access to finance and infrastructure, labor skills, and corruption. Different aspects of regulation have varying degrees of economic importance depending on countries' income levels, legal regimes, and other characteristics. Seven of DB's 10 indicators presume that lessening regulation is always desirable, whether a country starts with a little or a lot of regulation. Reform as measured by the DB indicators typically means reducing regulations and their burden, irrespective of their potential benefits.

The evaluation confirmed that the DB indicators primarily measure laws and regulations as they are written. But the relevance of each indicator in a given country depends on the extent to which the law is actually applied, which DB does not aim to measure. Likewise, the pay-off of a particular regulatory reform will depend on how significant a burden the regulation poses in practice. These limitations underscore the need for DB to be interpreted cautiously and used in conjunction with complementary tools such as Investment Climate Assessments.

Overall, the indicators objectively and reliably measure what they set out to measure, with a few qualifications. The controversial *employing workers* indicator is consistent with the letter of relevant International Labor Organization (ILO) conventions, but not always their spirit, insofar as it gives lower scores to countries that have chosen policies for greater job protection. Systematic differences in the country rankings for a few indicators are associated with countries' legal origins in civil or common law, but these patterns have little impact on the overall rankings or the validity of the exercise. The *paying taxes* indicator includes an anomalous subindicator— the *total tax rate*—which does not simply measure administrative burden to firms, but rather reflects a country's overall fiscal policy derived from social preferences. Finally, inaccurate nomenclature and overstated claims of the indicators' explanatory power have provoked considerable criticism from stakeholders.

Methodology and Data Reliability

DB collects its information from expert informants in each country, mostly lawyers, who provide information free of charge. This process can generate reliable data, but three areas of vulnerability need to be addressed.

First, the data are provided by few informants, with some data points for a country generated by just one or two firms. Of particular concern is the *paying taxes* indicator—DB relies exclusively on a single firm to provide both the underlying methodology and the data for 142 countries. The number and diversity of informants for all indicators need to be increased and their information validated more systematically. An increase in the informant base will require a systematic vetting process to reduce self-selection bias. Simplifying

the questionnaire may also help to encourage more informants to contribute.

Second, although DB makes available a great deal of information about its data and methods, it remains insufficiently transparent about the number and types of informants for each indicator, the adjustments its staff make to the data received from informants, and the changes made to previously published data and their effects on the rankings. DB needs to adequately explain to users the possibilities for errors and biases.

Third, DB makes much of its country rankings. The rankings entail three weaknesses. First, because most of the indicators presume that less regulation is better, it is difficult to tell whether the top-ranked countries have good and efficient regulations or simply inadequate regulation. Second, the small informant base makes it difficult to measure confidence in the accuracy of the individual indicator values, and thus in the aggregate rankings. Third, changes in a country's ranking depend importantly on where it sits on the distribution: small changes can produce large ratings jumps, and vice versa. These factors contribute to anomalies in the rankings.

These issues alone may not jeopardize the DB indicators' reliability. But the lack of transparency about them undermines DB's credibility and goodwill. DB's documents and presentations should include full explanations and cautions on these points.

Motivating and Designing Reforms

The DB indicators have motivated policy makers to discuss and consider business regulation issues. Its active dissemination in easy-to-understand language permits widespread press coverage and generates interest from businesses, nongovernmental organizations (NGOs), and senior policy makers.

DB has had less influence on the choice, scope, and design of reforms. Most Bank Group staff and country stakeholders interviewed for this evaluation report that they draw on a range of analytical material to determine the nature, sequence, and direction of reforms; the DB indicators have limited use in this regard. As a cross-country benchmarking exercise, DB cannot be expected to capture the country-specific considerations involved in prioritizing, sequencing, and designing policy reforms. Each year DB spotlights countries that have demonstrated the largest gain in the overall ranking and an improvement on at least three indicators. Such an approach, while transparent, does not capture the reforms' relevance and their potential impact on the binding constraints to the investment climate in the country.

IEG did not find evidence that the DB indicators have distorted policy priorities in the countries or in the Bank Group's programs, or that countries have made superficial changes for the sole purpose of improving their rankings.

In summary, DB measures the costs but not the benefits of regulation. Despite its methodological limitations, it has contributed to development by providing countries with a basis for international comparisons of their regulatory regimes. It has helped to catalyze debates and dialogue about investment climate issues in developing countries. For the Bank Group, it is a key global knowledge product. Most of the methodological limitations can and should be addressed promptly, lest they undermine its credibility. Inaccurate nomenclature should be rectified and the DB reports should not overstate claims of causality and the indicators' explanatory power.

Implications for the Bank Group

The evaluation notes two broader implications for the Bank Group.

First, the Bank Group, by prominently recognizing DB's highly ranked countries, may inadvertently be signaling that it values reduced regulatory burdens more than other development goals. The Bank Group's approach entails helping countries achieve a wide range of objectives, yet it has no comparable way of celebrating improvements in other important development outcomes.

Second, the DB exercise has demonstrated that cross-country ranking can be effective in spurring dialogue and motivating interest and action. It could potentially be applied to other development issues—those for which actionable indicators can serve as proxies for the target outcomes and for which the direction of improvement is uniform for all countries.

Recommendations

1. **To improve the credibility and quality of the rankings, the DB team should:**
   a. **Take a strategic approach** to selecting and increasing the number of informants:
      - Establish and disclose selection criteria for informants.
      - Focus on the indicators with fewest informants and on countries with the least reliable information.
      - Formalize the contributions of the supplemental informants by having them fill out the questionnaire.
      - Involve Bank Group staff more actively to help identify informants.
   b. **Be more transparent** about the following aspects of the process:
      - *Informant base*: Disclose the number of informants for each indicator at the country level, differentiating between those who complete questionnaires and those who provide supplemental information.
      - *Changes in data*: Disclose all data corrections and changes as they are made. Explain their effect on the rankings, and, to facilitate research, make available all previously published data sets.
      - *Use of the indicators:* Be clear about the limitations in the use of the indicators for a broader policy dialogue on a country's development priorities.
   c. **Revise the *paying taxes* indicator to include only measures of administrative burden.** Since the tax rate is an important part of the business climate, DB should continue to collect and present simple information on corporate tax rates, but exclude it from the rankings (as it does for information on nonwage

labor costs in the *employing workers* indicator). A wider range of informants should also be engaged for the *paying taxes* indicator.

2. **To make its reform analysis more meaningful, the DB team should:**

a. **Make clear that DB measures improvements to regulatory costs and burdens,** which is only one dimension of any overall reform of the investment climate.

b. **Trace the impact of DB reforms at the country level.** The DB team should work with country units to analyze the effects of implementing the reforms measured by the DB indicators (such as revised legislation or streamlined processes) on: (i) firm performance, (ii) perceptions of business managers on related regulatory burdens, and (iii) the efficiency of the regulatory environment in the country.

3. **To plan future additions or modification to the indicators, the DB team should:**

a. **Use Bank analyses to drive the choice of DB indicators.** Business Enterprise Surveys, Investment Climate Assessments, and other work can help determine stakeholders' priorities for domestic private sector growth. The DB team should use such analyses to determine the choice of new indicators and periodically reassess its current set of indicators.

b. **Pilot and stabilize the methodology before including new indicators in rankings.** Frequent changes in methodology make comparison across time less meaningful. New indicators should be piloted (that is, data collected and published for comment, but not factored into the rankings) until the methodology is validated and stabilized.

Management Response

Management welcomes this Independent Evaluation Group (IEG) review of the World Bank/International Finance Corporation (WB/IFC) Doing Business (DB) indicators. It notes the finding that the DB exercise has been effective in motivating interest, spurring dialogue on reforms, and stimulating action. Suggestions and recommendations in the review will be used to strengthen the DB process going forward. That said, management has a set of observations it would like to make on the analysis. Specific responses to IEG's recommendations are given in the attached Management Action Record table.

Concurrence with the Broad Thrust of the Analysis and Recommendations

The evaluation contains a number of important conclusions that management finds most helpful. Specifically, these include:

- An acknowledgement that the DB exercise has been highly effective in spurring dialogue on reforms and motivating interest and action. It has also informed a large academic literature on regulatory reform and the impact of regulation on economic and social outcomes (nearly 800 academic articles as of June 2007). Such research can aid policy makers, particularly in developing countries, in the search for the optimal kind and level of regulation to ensure that the majority of the population can participate in economic activity and benefit from legal certainty and social protection.
- The recommendation to apply similar benchmarking to other development issues and to encourage the development of actionable cross-country indicators that can track improvements over time.
- The finding that while effective in catalyzing reforms debates and dialogue, the DB indicators have not distorted policy priorities or encouraged policy makers to make superficial changes to improve rankings.
- The conclusion that the DB *employing work-ers* index complies with the core labor standards and all other relevant conventions of the International Labor Organization.
- The conclusion that the legal origin, whether civil or common law, does not determine a country's score in the DB indicators. A hypothetical civil law economy based on best practices would rank third in the global ease of doing business.
- Concrete suggestions on improving the transparency of the data collection and analysis and the respondent selection process.
- A recommendation to use other World Bank analyses, most importantly the Enterprise Surveys and Investment Climate Assessments, to inform the choice of topics in DB and enrich the analysis in future reports.
- A concrete proposal on piloting methodologies on new indicators before including them in the aggregate ranking on the ease of doing business.

Management Observations

Management has four issues that it would like to raise with regard to the analysis and recommendations in this review.

Paying Taxes Indicator. The IEG review recommends revising the *paying taxes* indicator to include only measures of administrative burden. In management's view, this recommendation is not consistent with another important recommendation, on the use of the other World Bank analyses to determine the priorities for regulatory reform. In the World Bank Enterprise Surveys, for example, tax rates are considered a top obstacle in twice as many countries as tax administration. In the Enterprise Surveys done in fiscal 2007, 17 of 40 find the tax rate to be among the top 3 obstacles, and 33 of 40 find it to be a bigger obstacle than tax administration. More generally, taxation is a regulatory tool and there is a trade-off between regulation and taxation. It is important to note that DB measures business taxes only, and therefore does not reflect the country's overall fiscal policy and revenue collection.

Making Available Previously Published Data sets. The IEG review recommends making available all previously published data sets, not corrected for errors and methodology changes. This practice is unorthodox and is not followed by other major primary data providers. Instead, DB follows the practice of other data providers and makes available back-calculated data series, corrected for errors and methodology changes. These data are made available on the "Get Full Data" page of the DB Web site. In addition, the data used in the background research for DB are published on the "Research" page of the DB Web site. These two data sources have been widely used by researchers, with more than 800 academic papers utilizing the DB data. Management agrees to make more information available on reasons for data changes to facilitate the distinction between methodological changes, systematic changes in coding rules, and errors. All methodology changes are described in detail on the Web site at http://www.doingbusiness.org/MethodologySurveys/. All revisions that affect the data published in the DB 2007 report integrated as of the time of publication of the DB 2008 report are being made available at the "Get Full Data" page of the Web site.

Increasing the Number of Respondents. The IEG review recommends increasing the number of DB respondents. Management notes that the DB methodology fundamentally depends on reading the text of laws and regulations. DB respondents provide references to the relevant texts of the laws and regulations. This is unlike the methodology of perceptions-based surveys, which depend on having large samples of representative respondents. To ensure accurate interpretation of regulations and time estimates, DB works with local experts who routinely administer or advise on legal and regulatory requirements. Since 2004, 10,270 local experts have contributed. Management agrees to further increase the respondent pool, and has taken action, including through visits to 151 countries. In addition, management has hired a respondents' manager as a member of the DB team to select and increase the number of respondents, focusing in particular on the poorest countries and other economies with the fewest number of respondents. Further, management commits to increase the involvement of Bank Group staff in recruiting respondents; to conduct annual data collection visits to the 50 economies with the fewest number of respondents; and to expand the piloted practice of giving out awards to the respondents who have contributed high-quality data over a sustained period of time.

Level of Regulation. The IEG review states that DB presumes less regulation is always better. This is incorrect. Six of the 10 indicators reward countries for having more regulation or a simplified way of implementing existing regulation. Top reformers in DB 2007 implemented stricter regulations (for example, China, Mexico, and Tanzania) or simplified their implementation (for example, Croatia, Guatemala, and Romania). The top 10 countries in the ease of doing business are Singapore, New Zealand, the United States, Hong Kong, Denmark, the United Kingdom, Canada, Ireland, Australia, and Iceland. Countries with no regulation receive a "no practice" score in the relevant area and the lowest ranking.

Conclusion

Overall, management welcomes this evaluation from IEG. Management generally accepts IEG's recommendations, with some caveats. Detailed responses to the recommendations are outlined in the attached Management Action Record.

Management Action Record

Recommendation	Management Response
To improve the credibility and quality of the rankings, the DB team should: (a) **Take a strategic approach** to selecting and increasing the number of informants: – Establish and disclose selection criteria for informants. – Focus on the indicators with fewest informants and countries with the least reliable information. – Formalize the contributions of the supplemental informants by having them fill out the questionnaire. – Involve Bank Group staff more actively to help identify informants. (b) **Be more transparent** on the following issues of process: – *Informant base*: Disclose the number of informants for each indicator at the country level, differentiating between those who complete questionnaires and those who provide "supplemental" information. – *Changes in data*: Disclose all data corrections and changes as they are made. Explain their effect on the rankings, and, to facilitate research, make available all previously published data sets. – *Use of the indicators*: Be clear about the limitations in the use of the indicators for a broader policy dialogue on a country's development priorities. (c) **Revise the *paying taxes* indicator to include only measures of administrative burden**. Since the tax rate is an important part of the business climate, DB should continue to collect and present simple information on corporate tax rates, but exclude it from the rankings (as it does for information on nonwage labor costs in the *employing workers* indicator). A wider range of informants should also be engaged for the *paying taxes* indicator.	**Mostly Agreed.** Bank Group management mostly agrees with this recommendation, noting that it primarily points to the importance of intensifying the rigor of recruiting and maintaining a large pool of expert respondents. – To implement the first part (point a) of this recommendation, management has hired a respondents' manager on the DB team. The task of the respondents' manager is to select and increase the number of respondents, focusing in particular on the poorest countries and other economies with the fewest number of respondents. In addition, management commits to increase the involvement of Bank Group staff in recruiting respondents and to conduct annual data collection visits to the 50 economies with the fewest number of respondents. Thirdly, management will expand the piloted practice of giving out awards to the respondents who have contributed high-quality data over a sustained period of time. Such awards serve to express gratitude for the respondents' efforts and to maintain the pool of respondents. – To implement the second part (point b) of this recommendation, management commits to disclosing the number of respondents for each indicator at the country level, starting with the launch of *Doing Business 2009*. Management is also making available details on data corrections/changes and methodology changes that have been made in the year following the launch of the previous report. Lastly, management commits to expanding the discussion on the limitations in the use of the DB indicators in the "Methodology" section of the report and on the Web site. However, management disagrees with the recommendation to make available all previously published data sets, not corrected for errors and methodology changes. This practice is unorthodox and is not followed by other major primary data providers. The data used in the background research for DB are already published on the "Research" page of the DB Web site. The full time series of DB data, corrected for errors and methodology changes, is also available at the "Get Full Data" page of the DB Web site. These two data sources have been widely used by researchers, with more than 800 academic papers utilizing the DB data. – Management mostly disagrees with the last point (point c) of the recommendation. The tax rate is often identified as a major constraint to business activity in the World Bank Enterprise Surveys. Including a measure of overall tax burden

Management Action Record

Recommendation	Management Response
	in the DB indicators provides a complete treatment for the topic of *paying taxes*. Focusing only on the administrative burden of *paying taxes* will take the DB methodology away from covering a broader spectrum of areas relevant to small domestic businesses. However, management commits to expand the range of respondents on the *paying taxes'* survey by recruiting a larger set of accounting and tax experts.
To make its reform analysis more meaningful, the DB team should: (a) **Make clear that DB measures improvements to regulatory costs and burdens,** which is only one dimension of any overall reform of the investment climate. (b) **Trace the impact of DB reforms at the country level.** The DB team should work with country units to analyze the effects of implementing the reforms measured by the DB indicators (such as revised legislation or streamlined process) on: (i) firm performance, (ii) perceptions of businessmen on related regulatory burdens, and (iii) the efficiency of the regulatory environment in the country.	**Agreed.** Bank Group management agrees with this recommendation and will strive to make it even clearer in future DB reports and presentations that DB covers only some dimensions of the overall reform of the investment climate. Management also commits to a measurement and evaluation agenda, in partnership with WB country units and IFC regional facilities, to document the effect of DB reforms on a set of economic and social indicators. The World Bank Enterprise Surveys in particular will be used for this work.
To plan future additions to or modifications of the indicators, the DB team should: (a) **Use Bank analyses to drive the choice of DB indicators.** Business Enterprise Surveys, Investment Climate Assessments, and other work can help determine stakeholders' priorities for domestic private sector growth. The DB team should use such analyses to determine the choice of new indicators, and periodically assess its current set of indicators. (b) **Pilot and stabilize the methodology before including new indicators in rankings.** Frequent changes in methodology make comparison across time less meaningful. New indicators should be piloted (that is, data collected and published for comment, but not factored into the rankings) until the methodology is validated and stabilized.	**Agreed.** Bank Group management agrees with this recommendation and will direct the DB team toward using other Bank Group analyses, and in particular the Enterprise Surveys and Investment Climate Assessments, for both determining the choice of new indicators and periodically assessing the existing set of DB indicators. Management also commits to publishing new sets of indicators in future DB reports for comment, while not factoring those in the rankings until their methodology is validated by academic research.

Chairperson's Summary: Committee on Development Effectiveness (CODE)

Background. The *Doing Business* (DB) report measures the burden of business regulation and ranks countries on 10 dimensions. The objective is to advance the private sector development agenda by motivating reforms via benchmarking; inform the design of reforms; enrich international initiatives on development effectiveness; and inform theory. This evaluation of the DB report takes an independent look at how indicators are constructed and what they measure.

IEG Main Findings. The evaluation finds DB indicators have been effective in drawing attention to the burdens of business regulation, but cannot capture other important dimensions of a county's business climate, the benefits of regulation, or related aspects of development. This underscores the need for DB to be interpreted cautiously and used in conjunction with complementary tools such as Investment Climate Assessments. The number and diversity of DB informants need to be increased and their information better validated. The DB should take a strategic approach to selecting and increasing informants; define and publish informant selection criteria; and be more transparent about its informant base and changes in data. DB assesses regulations as they are written, not the extent or way in which they are applied. The DB reports should not overstate the indicators' explanatory power. The total tax rate subindicator goes beyond administrative burden to also reflect a country's fiscal policy choices. Thus IEG recommends that the DB exclude it from the calculation of the aggregate ranking but continue to collect and publish this important information. The DB team routinely changes a large share of the data after it has been published and

posted on the Web site; it should acknowledge that its published data are subject to change and make available to researchers all versions of the data set. The DB makes much of annual changes in country rankings, but these need to be understood in context. The DB team should make clear that DB measures reductions in regulatory costs and tracks reforms at the country level, but is not a general indicator of investment climate quality. Lastly, the DB team should use Bank analyses to inform the development of further DB indicators, and should pilot and stabilize methodology before including new indicators.

Draft Management Response. Management welcomed the evaluation of the DB report, noting its acknowledgement that the DB exercise has been highly effective in spurring dialogue and action on reforms, and the recommendation that similar benchmarking be applied to other development issues. Management highlighted three issues in the IEG recommendations. IEG recommends that DB revise the *paying taxes* indicator to include only administrative burden measures and continue to collect and present information on the tax rate but exclude it from the rankings.

However, management finds that this is not consistent with IEG's recommendation on use of Enterprise Surveys and Investment Climate Assessments to determine regulatory reform priorities, as Enterprise Surveys regularly identify the tax burden as a major concern to entrepreneurs. IEG recommends making available all previously published data sets to facilitate research, which in management's view would be unorthodox; in this context management also notes that back-calculated data series, adjusted for methodology changes and correction, are made available on the DB Web site. Management agrees with IEG's recommendation to increase DB informants, and is actively engaged in this area.

DGE Statement. DB is a widely recognized product of the World Bank Group (WBG) and a prominent part of its work on private sector development. Being a rating exercise, DB has also generated important questions and concerns. Just as it is important to disseminate what the DB indicators do, it is important to note what the DB indicators do not do. While measuring the regulatory burden that some firms in the formal sector face, it does not capture some of the most crucial variables affecting the investment climate of a country, such as macroeconomic stability, labor skills, access to credit, infrastructure, or corruption. Going further, they do not touch on the social or economy-wide benefits that regulations yield, such as safety, environmental protection, or worker protection. While a useful measure of the burden of legal regulations, they are not and should not be used as an index of the quality of a country's business climate.

Overall Conclusions and Next Steps. CODE members welcomed the IEG evaluation of the DB report as well as the Draft Management Response. Overall, members welcomed the IEG review of the DB indicators and commended the quality of the report. While noting that the DB report cannot capture all dimensions of a country's business climate, some members acknowledged its contributions in promoting reforms in some countries. Members raised a wide set of comments—among them: DB is work in progress; the DB report should clarify what indicators are *not* intended to measure; DB can help governments improve their investment environment; DB needs a clear communication strategy to the public and use of disclaimers; the indicators may promote regulations but do not capture effective enforcement of the rules; there was recognition that DB indicators help to highlight the importance of regulations; IEG found some weaknesses in DB methodology that management should address; avoid using DB as ranking of countries that may have an impact on resource allocations; and take note that benchmarks and regulations are not unique to DB—as well as questions on how functional equivalence can be taken into account across common-law countries versus civil-law countries.

Most members agreed with IEG's recommendations for DB to take a strategic approach to selecting and increasing the number of informants. There were other comments on the methodology of DB: the need to look not only at what the DB indicators do not do, but rather focus on what they do; there should be emphasis on reliability of indicators; and the indicators should capture country advances or effective reforms. Some members cautioned against the use of DB indicators to top-rank countries. They questioned how to look at rankings. One member suggested including cost of regulations of FDI and DB indicators and to consider subnational governments' regulations. Another member felt the DB indicators do not lead to necessary reform and do not consider the political economy, and questioned the work of the DB indicators. On the *paying taxes* indicator, there were diverse views expressed by speakers, as some do not agree with IEG's recommendations to exclude tax rate from the indicator. Others questioned the rationale for including the tax rate as part of the *paying taxes* indicator. On the *employing workers* indicator, some speakers noted that it may overstate what it measures.

One member suggested disclosing the DB report together with the IEG review. Management stated that it has taken note of comments and suggestions raised during the meeting.

The following main issues were raised at the meeting:

IEG Evaluation and DB Report. Several members welcomed the IEG evaluation of the DB indicators. A member suggested it be published as part of, or alongside, the DB report. *Management commented that publishing the evaluation with the report, and doing so annually, would not be the most practical approach.* A speaker proposed that the IEG evaluation be featured on the DB Web site. *IEG confirmed that there would be active dissemination of the DB evaluation.* Several members noted DB had spurred debate and has been helpful in improving regulatory environments. At the same time, some members remarked that the DB report had shortcomings and that it was a work in progress. A member wondered how DB had become a flagship document if so many shortcomings existed, while a speaker queried as to the quality checks needed to launch a WBG product. One member noted that for small states, this was a very good tool, allowing countries to assess their business environment. A speaker added that DB was a product that people wanted to read, understand, and apply.

DB Indicators. A member stated that the methodology behind the DB indicators needed clarification, while the indicators had to be simple and easy to understand. *Management noted that one of the fundamental objectives of DB was to continuously improve indicators to make them relevant and accurate.* Another member made the case that there was no need to continue to produce DB and suggested that comparative studies on regulation issues be emphasized. A speaker commented that DB needed to be clearer as to how an indicator reflects specific outcomes (i.e., registering a business vs. number of licenses), as some indicators have issues related to health and safety. *Management noted that the indicators do not claim to measure all aspects of the business environment, and that the decision to keep DB relatively focused was in keeping with an earlier Board discussion. Management agreed that it is important to keep improving the description of what the indica-*

tors measure. The DGE commented that the DB indicators had sparked constructive debate among country authorities and business interests, while also provoking fears that it may distort policy priorities among country authorities and in the WBG by emphasizing the private costs of regulation at the expense of social benefits.

A member noted that perhaps the IEG report was underestimating DB users (i.e., policy makers), as they do not necessarily read DB as a document that promotes "no regulations." In that sense, he added that policy makers use the DB report when developing policy and can compare with countries that have implemented similar regulations. *Management agreed that policy makers are faced with a wide range of stakeholders they have to respond to and should not be underestimated. IEG noted that the evaluation finds that policy makers used DB as one tool among others in developing policy reforms. The DB reports should avoid claiming that specific reforms were directly stimulated by the DB indicators. IEG further recommends that the DB team work with country teams to trace the impact of country-level reforms measured by the DB indicators.* One member asked that the DB indicators not be used in Bank operations, particularly resource allocation, while another member noted that since these are partial indicators they should be used with prudence. A member noted that Operations Policy and Country Services should look into how IEG's evaluations can affect the use of the DB indicators in the CPIA exercise. *Management noted that for background information, the CPIA draws on a number of data sets, each of which covers only some aspects of economic performance.*

Regulation vs. Deregulation. A member commented that improved indicators may not necessarily lead to correct reforms since they are designed with the assumption that the lighter the regulation, the better. *Management clarified that the DB report does not reject regulation; instead it is the issues of quality and efficiency of rules that are the focus of the DB report. IEG noted that their evaluation supports* that policy makers use the DB indicators sensibly and in tandem with other data. One member observed that the tension that exists with regulations that can either be promoted by rent-seekers or to protect the public interest is always present. *The DGE observed that the WBG has the responsibility to emphasize both the importance of efficiency in implementing regulations as well as their potential value added.*

Disclaimer and Transparency. Several members noted the importance of communicating what the DB report measures. A member remarked that DB was not a business-climate ranking or indicator and that it was important to communicate (i.e., disclaimer) the meaning of these regulatory indicators. *Management added that it was very important for the Bank to communicate what it is that we are measuring and what we are not.* Some speakers noted that they would like clear disclaimers and comments on the social value of good regulation. *Management remarked that the DB report has a "health warning." It added that it would look to further explain that deregulation is not the main purpose of the DB report.*

Regulation Enforcement and Impact. A few members commented that indicators measuring regulation effectiveness must also measure impact on the ground. *Management noted that the DB report not only looks at the level of regulation but also at the compliance cost and how this affects local entrepreneurs. It also added that there is a dimension of enforcement and implementation that is being observed by comparing DB data with data from the Enterprise Surveys, which capture the experience of actual business owners.*

Country Rankings. Some members noted that country rankings needed further work, as a change in rankings does not necessarily improve the regulatory environment, thus making the exercise arbitrary. *Management commented that in some cases the DB indicators look for more regulation (i.e., protecting investors); while other indicators will give the lowest*

ranking if you have no regulation (i.e., property registry). *IEG pointed out that the introduction of the "Reformer's Club" in the DB marketing clearly signals a normative interpretation to the rankings.* A member added that countries have varied constraints (e.g. scarce resources, limited capacity), and these may be exacerbated by competition to improve rankings. He further added that the Bank is not in a position to rank its members. *Management noted that countries have used the indicators constructively, while also taking into account quality issues and country-specific limitations.*

One member asked that the request to withdraw the rankings should be seriously considered. Another member suggested that a best practice component could be added, while another member noted that benchmarks are not unique to DB and are part of a wave of international standards. A speaker observed that measurements for these rankings change after the release of the DB report. *Management added that when comparing the exercise to a similar evaluation at the OECD (i.e., Product Market Regulation for OECD Countries), in the case of regulatory complexity and costs, the OECD and DB rankings are highly correlated. IEG noted that improvement in DB country rankings should not be characterized as improvements in the business climate; rather, they should be interpreted as a partial indicator of a reduction in the regulatory burden.*

Paying Taxes Indicator. A few members noted that the tax rate issue was an important one to flag and should be considered. A member noted that it would be useful to retain the tax rate as part of the *paying taxes* indicator, while another member commented that the term "total tax" was misleading. *IEG noted that the reliance on a sole source for information underlying the paying taxes indicator is risky. IEG recommends that DB continue to gather and publish important information about taxes that firms pay, but discontinue factoring this into the overall rankings. IEG commented that depending on a country's resources and fiscal requirements,* lowering taxes could prove to be negative for the investment climate, and indirectly for individual firms. A member stressed that the tax system should be taken in its totality to evaluate the associated burden or ease for undertaking business in a country. A speaker disagreed with the proposed changes to the *paying taxes* indicator, as tax remains one of the major business constraints for business development (i.e., in the Africa Region) and argued that focusing only on the administrative burden of paying taxes will weaken the DB methodology. Another speaker noted that the issue was not the tax rate per se, but at which threshold it became a burden to business activity. *Management noted that it did not agree with excluding the tax rate. It noted that in the Enterprise Surveys, one of the issues most raised by business owners is the tax burden.*

Employing Workers Indicator. A few speakers thought that the WBG should encourage countries to guarantee internationally recognized worker rights and that DB should look to reflect certain labor standards (e.g., collective bargaining, forced labor). *Management noted that the employing workers indicator is consistent with ILO standards. IEG noted that there are anomalies in the employing workers ranking, as the top country is Singapore, with very good regulations, while the Marshall Islands, with no regulations, is second.* A speaker commented that no one would confuse Singapore with the Marshall Islands when it comes to labor market regulation. *Management noted that by focusing on the regulatory costs associated with employing workers, this indicator provides a basis for analysis of how regulation relates to important outcomes such as informality or higher levels of women or youth employed. In that sense, a DB indicator triggers a conversation about a range of issues related to it. Management added that*

ongoing DB work is focusing on issues related to potential gender discrimination.

Increasing Informants. Members noted that management should use a strategic approach to selecting and increasing the number of informants (e.g., accounting, tax experts) for DB. A few speakers added that these should include relevant stakeholders (e.g., employers, consumers). *IEG commented that DB should disclose how many informants are the sources for each indicator, and that the reliability of the ratings would improve if this number were increased.*

Nomenclature. Speakers noted that titles for DB indicators should more clearly reflect what they are measuring. *IEG recommended that the DB report be precise in the language used to describe what is being measured, as the names of the many indicators may overstate the scope of their coverage. In the case of employing workers, it covers specific rules about the hiring and firing of workers and hours of work, but does not cover other critical areas (e.g., union rights, child labor).*

New Indicators and Subnational Regulation. A member suggested including the cost of regulations on foreign direct investment within DB. *Management noted that it was in the early stages of piloting a foreign direct investment indicator. IEG and management agreed that it is important to pilot-test and validate new methodologies before introducing any new indicators.* A member proposed that subnational government regulation be looked into. *Management agreed with the idea of looking into subnational-level regulation (i.e., across cities) and noted that it already has such a program and now covers over 200 cities globally with subnational reports.*

Giovanni Majnoni
Acting Chairman

Chapter 1

Evaluation Highlights

- The Doing Business (DB) indicators provide consistent cross-country data annually on 10 specific aspects of a country's regulatory framework.
- DB indicators are based on research that associates better regulations with an improved investment climate, and thence with economic growth—but this research is still nascent.
- Seven DB indicators presume that less regulation is better.
- Five emphasize aspects of debt enforceability and availability of collateral.
- DB argues that regulatory reform will encourage informal businesses to formalize.
- DB indicators do not aim to capture the potential benefits of regulation. Users must be mindful of what the DB indicators measure and what they do not.

Woman standing outside restaurant, Keur Moussa, Senegal. Photo reproduced by permission of Philippe Lissac/Godong/Corbis.

The Ideas Behind
the Indicators

This chapter situates the DB indicators in the context of investment climate and private sector development. It introduces the main principles that shape what the indicators measure and how they are constructed.

Role of the Investment Climate in Private Sector Growth

Private sector growth is essential for developing countries to create jobs and raise incomes. The rate and nature of private sector growth in a country is affected by many factors, including macroeconomic and political stability, traditions and culture, physical infrastructure, availability of capital, and human resources. Institutional, policy, and regulatory factors also play an important role. They are often grouped together under the rubric of "investment climate," as depicted in figure 1.1.

DB measures selected aspects of the investment climate—namely, the laws and regulations governing how firms do business (see shaded areas of figure 1.1). Research suggests, broadly speaking, that the regulatory framework does matter for economic outcomes, but it is inconclusive about which regulations matter most, and how much they matter compared with other determinants (Dollar, Hallward-Dreimeier, and Mengistae 2005).

Business laws and regulations are intended to generate benefits to society at large, but they also inevitably impose costs on the individual firm. Some regulations on firms may deliver an important public good—for example, the prohibi-

tion of child labor. Others—such as requiring multiple official stamps on a document—deliver little or no public benefit. They simply provide officials with opportunities for rent-seeking. The policy maker's challenge is to find the level of regulation where the desired level of public good—say, tax revenues or worker safety—can be obtained with the minimum loss of efficiency to affected firms. Some countries may be over-regulated; others may be under-regulated. The level of regulation in any country should reflect a country's preferred trade-off between public goods and private (firm) benefits (see box 1.1).

Substantial research literature has established an association between the characteristics of the business regulatory environment and the performance of firms, and thence to macroeconomic outcomes (see Acemoglu and Johnson 2005; Botero and others 2004; Djankov and others 2002; Hall and Jones 1999; Kaufmann 2002; Kaufmann and Ziodo-Lobaton 1999; Kaufmann, Kray, and Mastruzzi 2006; Knack and Keefer 1995; Rodrik 2004). DB's Web site contains a comprehensive bibliography of this research, to which the DB team itself has contributed.[1] Generally, this work uses cross-country comparisons to show that various proxy indicators for governance or business regulation are associated with the size or performance of

The DB indicators are premised on research that associates characteristics of the investment climate with growth, and the effects of laws and regulation on the investment climate.

Figure 1.1: DB Measures Selected Aspects of Investment Climate

Stability and security	Regulation and taxation	Finance and infrastructure	Workers and labor markets
Stability • Reduce political instability from civil wars, political conflict, etc. • Maintain macroeconomic stability with low inflation, sustainable budget deficits, and realistic exchange rates **Security of property rights** • Reduce robbery, fraud, and other crimes against property • End uncompensated expropriation of property • Verify rights to land and other property • Facilitate contract enforcement	**Regulation** • Balance market and government failures for a good institutional fit • Address regulatory cost and informality • Reduce uncertainty and risk in interpretation and implementation of existing regulations • Reduce regulatory barriers to competition **Taxation** • Broaden tax base • Increase autonomy of tax agencies • Reduce corruption in tax administration • Confront informality • Simplify tax structure • Improve customs administration • Improve compliance through computerization	**Finance** • Foster competition in the banking sector • Control risk-taking by banks and other financial institutions • Secure rights of borrowers, creditors, and shareholders • Improve credit information by using credit bureaus and stronger data protection and credit-reporting laws **Infrastructure** • Improve climate for investment in infrastructure by securing investors' property rights, fostering competition, and encouraging private participation • Improve public management of infrastructure	• Foster a skilled and healthy workforce by expanding access to education, improving education quality, supporting life-long learning, and the like • Help workers affected by large-scale restructurings by reinforcing social insurance mechanisms and reaching out to the large share of workers in rural and informal economies • Craft labor market interventions to benefit all (formal and informal) in the process of setting wages, regulation of working conditions, and hiring and firing of workers

Source: World Bank 2004.
Note: Shaded areas are those the DB indicators attempt to measure.

the private sector or overall macroeconomic outcomes.[2]

Business is affected not only by laws and regulations, but also by a host of other variables outside the scope of the DB indicators. The Bank's Investment Climate Assessments (ICAs) and Business Enterprise Surveys and the World Economic Forum's Global Competitiveness Reports ask business leaders to rank the most important constraints they face. In this evaluation's 13 case study countries, these assessments note 12 important constraints (see table 1.1).[3] Business leaders most often mentioned

Box 1.1: A Good Investment Climate Balances Private and Societal Interests

The *World Development Report 2005: A Better Investment Climate for Everyone*, addressed the trade-offs between private and social interests:

At the heart of the problem lies a basic tension. . . . Most firms complain about taxes, but taxes finance public services that benefit the investment climate and other social goals. Many firms would also prefer to comply with fewer regulations, but sound regulation addresses market failures

and can therefore improve the investment climate and protect other social interests [p. 6].

A good investment climate is not just about generating profits for firms—if that were the goal, the focus could be limited to minimizing costs and risks. A good investment climate improves outcomes for society as a whole. That means that some costs and risks are properly borne by firms [p. 2].

access to and/or cost of financing, corruption, lack of infrastructure, inefficient government bureaucracy, and tax rates. Four of these 12 constraints are reflected in the DB indicators: inefficient government bureaucracy (that can include regulatory constraints); tax rates and tax administration; and restrictive labor regulations.[4] Interviews with Bank Group staff and stakeholders broadly confirm this analysis: they rated lack of infrastructure, access to and cost of credit, and a shortage of human capital as the three most important constraints to private sector development.[5]

The DB indicators—confined as they are to a subset of these factors—do not and cannot be expected to identify priority action areas across the business climate as a whole. For example, in low-income and post-conflict countries, such as Burundi, political insecurity was an overarching constraint. As a standardized cross-country data set, the DB indicators also cannot elicit any one country's idiosyncratic issues. Nor can the DB indicators be expected to help determine policy actions, because they cannot situate the regulatory constraints within a country's policy context and macroeconomic framework. ICAs and other surveys are better suited to playing both these roles.

But research overall is inconclusive about the direction of causation. While it is typically hypothesized that better regulations spur better economic results, causality may also run the opposite way, insofar as citizens in more advanced economies demand more efficient regulations. There may also be unidentified causal factors. For example, if cross-country analysis finds that higher labor productivity is associated with less onerous business start-up procedures, it may be that a third factor (such as the quality of human capital) is driving indica-

Investment decisions also depend on other variables not measured by the DB indicators— notably, the cost and access to finance and infrastructure and labor skills.

Table 1.1: DB Covers Only Some of the Top Constraints to Business (Constraints mentioned by business leaders; those in bold are covered by DB)

Top constraints	World Bank Group Investment Climate Assessments and Enterprise Surveys;[a] Global Competitiveness Report[b]
Access and/or cost of financing[c]	Algeria, Burundi, China, Moldova, Nigeria, Rwanda, Tanzania, Vietnam
Corruption	Albania, Algeria, Burundi, China, Moldova, Mongolia, Nigeria, Vietnam
Inefficient government bureaucracy[d]	Albania, Algeria, China, Moldova, Mongolia, Netherlands, Peru, Spain
Infrastructure (such as electricity, transportation)	Albania, Netherlands, Nigeria, Rwanda, Tanzania, Vietnam
Tax rates	Albania, Moldova, Mongolia, Rwanda, Spain, Tanzania
Tax administration	Burundi, Mongolia, Peru
Anticompetitive or informal practices[d]	Albania, Peru, Spain
Restrictive labor regulations	Netherlands, Spain
Skills and education of available workers	Spain, Vietnam
Political instability	Burundi, Peru
Macroeconomic instability	Moldova
Economic and regulatory policy uncertainty	Peru

Sources: World Bank Investment Climate Assessments and Business Enterprise Surveys (2004–07); World Economic Forum 2007/08.

Note: Management notes that tax rates are the fifth most widely cited constraint by businesses. This highlights the importance of having a measure of tax burden in the *paying taxes* indicator. In all World Bank Enterprise Surveys done since 2006, 17 of 40 find the tax rate to be among the top 3 obstacles and 33 of 40 find them to be a bigger obstacle than tax administration.

a. Respondents were given a list of 18 factors and asked to rate them on a scale of 1 to 5: 0 = no obstacle, 1 = minor obstacle, 2 = moderate obstacle, 3 = major obstacle, and 4 = very severe obstacle. The top three factors—with the most respondents commenting that the factor was either a major obstacle or very severe obstacle—are displayed in the table.

b. Respondents were given a list of 14 factors and asked to select the 5 most problematic for doing business in their country and to rank them between 1 (most problematic) and 5. Responses were weighted according to their ranking. The top 3 constraints by country are displayed in the table.

c. Includes several factors, such as access to banking and credit services, interest rates, as well as availability of collateral as measured by the DB indicators.

d. Constraint is not offered as a potential response in one of the surveys.

tors for economic performance and quality of public administration in the same direction (based on Altenburg and von Drachenfels 2006).

Research affirms associations between outcomes and the regulatory environment...

Recent research has begun to test the links between the DB indicators and economic outcomes, although this research has been constrained by DB's short time series. Djankov, McLiesh, Ramalho, and Shleifer (2008) looked at reforms in *getting credit,* and found that credit rises after improvements in creditor rights and information. Commander and Svejnar (2007)[6] found little evidence that the DB indicators have a robust relationship with business environment constraints and firm performance, as measured by revenue efficiency.[7]

...but suggests a need for caution in attributing economic outcomes to changes in DB indicators.

A background paper commissioned for this evaluation (Commander and Tinn 2007) found no statistically significant relationships between the 2004 DB indicators and growth rates. It found few significant relationships with intermediate outcomes.[8] For example, better legal rights for creditors and debtors were positively associated with private credit, capital inflows, and foreign direct investment, but not with private bank credit. There was a weak association between investment and *dealing with licenses* and *enforcing contracts.* No significant association emerged between *registering property* and construction, *trading across borders* and exports and imports, *starting a business* and the size of the informal economy, or *employing workers* and employment.

Seven of the 10 DB indicators exhibit a preference for less regulation—3 most notably: employing workers, paying taxes, and dealing with licenses.

Finally, a recent analysis found no significant relationship between reforms as measured by changes in the DB indicators and aggregate investment and unemployment rates (Eiffert 2007). Because of the relative newness of DB data, as well as other limitations described in chapter 2, this research cannot be considered definitive, but it suggests a need to be cautious in attributing economic outcomes to changes in the DB indicators.

Three Principles Underlying What DB Measures

The DB model is anchored in the research described above that associates firm performance and economic growth with characteristics of the regulatory environment.[9] DB puts these associations into a normative framework by selecting 10 categories of laws and regulations to be measured, devising a procedure (discussed in chapter 2) for rating and ranking countries, and deriving diagnoses and recommendations for policy makers to use (see chapter 4).

The content of the DB indicators as a group embodies three important ideas:

1. **Less regulation is preferable** across all parts of the distribution and in all countries.[10] The ratings do not allow for a minimum desirable level of regulation needed to ensure public benefits. This principle is embedded in 7 of the 10 indicators[11] and is especially prominent in the following 3 indicators:[12]

   Employing workers: The fewer the restrictions on hours of work and the more easily a firm can lay off redundant workers, the better the ranking. The 10 top-ranked countries include 5 developed countries with high-quality labor laws, but also 5 small island states, some with inadequate labor protections (see box 3.6). Thus the indicator cannot capture the possible offsetting benefits of job protection.

   Dealing with licenses: The fewer the steps needed to get a permit to construct a building,[13] the higher the score. Possible benefits from safety and environmental checks are not considered.

   Paying taxes: The lower the overall tax rate as a share of a firm's profit, the higher the score. Among the 10 top-rated countries on this indicator are Maldives, Oman, Singapore, and the United Arab Emirates. Each of these has special characteristics that make it an unsuitable role model for other countries seeking an optimal level of corporate taxation (see box 3.5 in chapter 3). For instance, Maldives derives almost all of its revenue from resort leases. The indicator overlooks each country's fiscal requirement to raise revenue, as well as the

Table 1.2: The 10 DB Indicators and Their Components

Indicator	Subindicators	Indicator	Subindicators
Starting a business	Procedures (number)	**Getting credit**	Strength of legal rights index (0–10)
	Time (days)		Depth of credit information index (0–6)
	Cost (% income per capita)		*Public registry coverage (% of adults)*
	Minimum capital (% income per capita)		*Private bureau coverage (% of adults)*
Dealing with licenses	Procedures (number)	**Enforcing contracts**	Procedures (number)
	Time (days)		Time (days)
	Cost (% income per capita)		Cost (% of claim)
Employing workers	Difficulty of hiring index (0–100)	**Trading across borders**	Documents to export (number)
	Rigidity of hours index (0–100)		Time to export (days)
	Difficulty of firing index (0–100)		Cost to export (US$ per container)
	Firing cost (weeks of salary)		Documents to import (number)
	Nonwage labor cost (% salary)		Cost to import (US$ per container)
			Time to import (days)
Registering property	Procedures (number)	**Paying taxes**	Payments (number per year)
	Time (days)		Time (hours per year)
	Cost (% of property value)		Total tax rate (% of profit)
Protecting investors	Extent of disclosure index (0–10)	**Closing a business**	Recovery rate (cents per dollar)
	Extent of director liability index (0–10)		*Time (years)*
	Ease of shareholder suits index (0–10)		*Cost (% of estate)*

Note: Italicized items are measured but not included in calculating the ease of doing business (EODB) ranking.

equity implications of alternative sources of revenue (Maldives government 2007).

Defining the point at which the costs of regulation exceed the benefits is difficult. It is likely that some developing countries impose more regulations than would be optimal for economic development. Some level of regulation is helpful for ensuring a supply of social goods such as health and safety, environmental protection, and transparency of business dealings. Regulations may even have benefits for individual firms—insofar as they ensure a level playing field with competitors, for example. Yet seven of the DB indicators, taken to their logical conclusion, would give the highest ranking to countries with the least regulation.[14]

2. **Property rights and debt enforceability are important determinants of lending and investment.** Five of the 10 indicators include measures of the en-forceability of debt contracts and availability of collateral.

Getting credit: The fewer the restrictions on what can be counted as collateral (and the more information lenders can obtain about borrowers' credit histories), the more likely lenders are to make loans and to be able to collect on them.

Enforcing contracts: The more efficiently the court system operates, the more easily a firm will be able to collect on a debt.

Registering property: The easier it is to register a property, the more likely the owner can use it as collateral for a loan, and the more likely the lender will collect on a bad loan.

Closing a business: The easier it is to close a business through formal bankruptcy (instead of simply ceasing operations), the greater the likelihood that creditors can collect on their loans.

Five of the 10 indicators measure the enforceability of debt contracts and availability of collateral, but leave out some factors that affect firms' use of credit.

Dealing with licenses: The easier it is to allow a constructed warehouse to be used as collateral, the higher the score.

DB's emphasis on collateral and debt enforceability derives in part from the work of Hernando de Soto, which posits that poor property owners are locked out of the formal economy because they lack legal rights to their land, so they cannot use it as collateral for loans to expand their businesses or improve their properties. De Soto's work, however, omits the many other factors that affect firms' actual use of credit, such as interest rates, value of the assets, degree of intermediation, culture, and the existence of viable entrepreneurial opportunities (see Galiani and Schargrodsky 2005; Commander and Tinn 2007). Peru's large-scale titling program, COFOPRI, did not induce the beneficiaries to solicit credit any more frequently than nonbeneficiaries, and credit applications from beneficiaries were turned down more frequently than those from nonbeneficiaries (Webb, Beuermann, and Revilla 2006). In Peru, lenders proved interested in the applicant's repayment capacity, not whether they had collateral, which often has low resale value (see Morris 2004).

The DB indicators argue that lighter regulation and less taxation encourage informal firms to move to the formal economy, but the literature is inconclusive about whether these factors can cause such change.

3. **Lighter regulation and taxation can encourage non-formal firms to shift into the formal economy.**

Starting a business: Simpler procedures to start a business will encourage informal enterprises to formalize.

Paying taxes: The easier the tax-paying procedures, the more likely a firm is to actually pay, rather than evade, taxes.

Employing workers: The fewer the restrictions on hours of work (within limits) and the more easily a firm can lay off redundant workers, the more likely it is that firms will employ workers on formal rather than on informal terms.

DB aims to provide policy makers with specific, actionable information.

The research literature is inconclusive about why the informal sector exists and persists. One explanation is simple tax avoidance. Another view is that people and firms in the informal economy face severe entry barriers caused by their low skills, lack of access to capital, isolated location, and other structural factors. A recent review noted that "Empirical studies show that only a very small number of micro-enterprises ever manage to upgrade and grow into larger units. The reasons are manifold. Micro-entrepreneurs may, for instance, lack information, technical skills, managerial competence, entrepreneurial spirit, and capital. . . . To graduate out of informality is thus a slow and difficult process of cultural change" (Altenburg and von Drachenfels 2006, p. 406).

DB focuses on the idea that excessive regulation of private sector activity inhibits the transition from the informal to the formal economy. Although some research shows that "countries with heavier entry regulation have lower firm entry and lower growth . . . there is very little evidence on the actual effects of business registration reform" (Bruhn 2007, p. 1). Recent research in Mexico finds that simplifying business registration procedures was associated with an increase in newly registered businesses, although the new business owners were formerly wage earners rather than unregistered business owners (Bruhn 2007).

Two Principles Underlying DB's Methodology

DB's methodology has two distinctive characteristics. It uses a set of discrete indicators to create an aggregate ranking, and it is applied exclusively to domestically owned firms in the formal sector.

Discrete and aggregable indicators

DB separately assesses discrete dimensions of the regulatory environment. This is aimed at providing policy makers with specific, actionable information. The 10 dimensions are not equally important in all countries. To illustrate:

- Protection of minority shareholders, as measured by *protecting investors*, was deemed less important in several client countries with more pressing constraints, such as lack of infrastructure and access to finance (see below).
- The rules measured by *employing workers* are

more important in countries with substantial formal employment and in countries with organized labor groups than in those where most people are small farmers.

This evaluation asked Bank Group staff and country stakeholders to rank the importance of the 10 DB indicators to private sector growth in their countries. While there were significant variations between countries, in aggregate over half the respondents rated eight dimensions as very important or important to the growth of the private sector in their countries. Only two indicators (*protecting investors* and *closing a business*) were found to be slightly important or not important by more than half the respondents interviewed.

The indicators themselves cannot capture country context, precisely because they are designed to allow cross-country comparisons on the basis of uniform criteria. By the same token, not all reforms will have an equal impact, and the DB indicators are not designed to identify within-country priorities. Users require supplemental information to determine the importance of each indicator or reform in a particular country setting. Stakeholders interviewed for the evaluation stressed the DB indicators' limitations in helping countries select priority reforms (see chapter 4).

DB aggregates country rankings for the 10 discrete elements, weighted equally, into a single composite ranking called the ease of doing business (EODB). Like any composite index, the EODB obscures its component information. The weights of the indicators are not important since the ranking does not change much with alternative weights.[15] Rather, the change in ranking for any country is driven largely by where a country is located on the distribution of countries on a specific indicator (discussed in chapter 2). Even within DB's own frame of reference, the composite indicator would more accurately (though less attractively) be named "index of regulatory burdens," since it does not capture all dimensions of doing business. (Other issues of nomenclature are discussed in chapter 3.)

The relevance of each indicator will necessarily vary by country.

Covers formal, domestically owned firms

The DB exercise gathers information about a particular subset of a country's private sector activity—the regula-tory environment facing domestically owned firms operating in the formal sector. The scope of this subset is defined by the specific information that informants are asked to provide (for example, what the law requires as distinct from what may actually happen) and the characteristics of the hypothetical firms in the stylized cases (for example, ownership, annual turnover, or minimum number of employees). The DB reports appropriately explain the scope and limitations of this coverage (World Bank-IFC 2007b, p. 67).

The DB reports explain the limitations of its approach.

Table 1.3: What DB Covers

DB includes	DB excludes
Small and medium-size firms[a]	Microenterprises and state-owned enterprises
Enterprises in the formal sector	Enterprises in the informal sector
Domestically owned firms and investors	Foreign-owned firms and foreign investors
Official and legal transactions and processes	Illegal, corrupt, informal, and out-of-court transactions and processes
Firms in the capital city	Firms outside the capital city
Limited liability companies	Sole proprietorships

a. The size of the firm varies, depending on the indicator. It ranges from 20 employees for *dealing with licenses,* 50 employees for *starting a business* and *registering property,* 60 employees for *paying taxes,* to more than 201 employees for *employing workers, trading across borders,* and *closing a business.* Three indicators (*getting credit, protecting investors,* and *enforcing contracts*) do not specify firm size.

Table 1.4: The Informal Economy Casts a Long Shadow

Region	Number of countries	Shadow economy[a] (% GDP)
Africa	24	41
Asia[b]	26	26
Latin America	17	41
Eastern Europe and Central Asia	23	38
OECD	21	17

Source: Schneider and Klinglmair 2004.

a. The shadow economy includes unreported income from production of legal and illegal goods and services, either for monetary or barter transactions.

b. This number is affected by the relatively low levels of informal activity in China (13.1 percent), Hong Kong (16.6 percent), Japan (11.3 percent), and Singapore (13.1 percent).

Some regulatory constraints are likely to be relatively unimportant for informal and microenterprises . . . DB's coverage explicitly excludes some types of enterprises and transactions (see table 1.3). Some of the laws and regulations that apply to small and medium-size domestically owned firms may well apply to other kinds of businesses, such as large-scale enterprises or those with foreign ownership. But the regulatory constraints that DB measures are likely to be relatively unimportant for informal and microenterprises, simply because they are more likely to conduct business without recourse to courts, formal credit providers, and taxes.

. . . which in some countries account for a significant share of private sector activity. In many countries, the informal sector accounts for a significant or even dominant share of private sector activity, especially in low- and middle-income countries (see table 1.4). Observers have criticized DB for not capturing the important constraints on nonformal and microenterprises. This observation, while true, is somewhat off the mark. As discussed above, DB is based on the view that informal firms and transactions should eventually enter the formal economy, and that this is more likely to occur if the burdens on firms in the formal sector are reduced.

In summary, the thrust of the DB is broadly consistent with credible research that more efficient business regulation is associated with better private sector performance, and thence macroeconomic outcomes. But the literature is necessarily partial, as it has not yet demonstrated the direction of causality. Furthermore, regulations deliver benefits as well as costs, and the policy choices countries make are necessarily based on the trade-offs between the two. What is good for a firm may not be good for firms as a group, or for the economy as a whole.

The DB exercise reflects these inherent trade-offs. As a cross-country comparison, DB is not intended to, and cannot, capture country nuances and nonlinear relationships. It notes the costs of regulation, but not the benefits.[16] Seven of DB's 10 indicators presume that reducing regulation is equally desirable whether a country starts with a little or a lot of regulation. While these limitations do not invalidate the exercise, they underscore the need to use the DB indicators cautiously and in conjunction with complementary tools, such as Investment Climate Assessments, when measuring a country's investment climate or related measures of development effectiveness.

Chapter 2

Evaluation Highlights

- DB collects its data largely from lawyers and accountants deemed knowledgeable about a country's laws and regulations.
- The number of informants who fill in questionnaires on any topic in a country is small.
- DB does not keep track of those who are invited but do not participate; thus participant bias cannot be estimated.
- The DB team validates and adjusts informants' data, which makes the data difficult to verify.
- DB regularly updates its data to reflect changes in methodology or correct errors, but previously published data sets are not made available to users, and the impact of such changes on the overall and indicator rankings is not stated.
- For a given amount of change in an indicator, a country's ranking may change a little or a lot, depending on its initial position in the ranking.

Workers in a furniture factory, Cotonou, Benin. Photo reproduced by permission of Jorgen Schytte/Still Pictures.

Collecting Information and Constructing the Rankings

Doing Business creates its annual country rankings using information supplied by persons deemed knowledgeable about selected laws and regulations in each country covered. The DB team identifies individual lawyers, notaries, officials, and firms and requests that they provide information on one or more specified DB topics. Since the process is not based on a survey sent to a large group, but rather on information solicited from selected individuals, the term "informants" is used in this evaluation instead of "respondents."

The validity of the DB indicators depends on how representative, reliable, and objective its process is for obtaining, recording, and analyzing information (see Dorbec 2006). This chapter assesses DB's processes for interviewing informants, reviewing and validating the information they supplied, and constructing the rankings.[1]

The Number of Informants

The 2007 and 2008 DB reports note that about 5,000 individuals provided information for the indicators. It is frequently the case that several individuals from the same firm or office help prepare the firm's response to the questionnaire. For example, junior staff may obtain data for a partner or principal to compile into the firm's written submission. The DB reports list each of these individuals as informants, but in this evaluation, each completed questionnaire is counted as one informant, irrespective of how many individuals helped to prepare it. Some of the listed individuals completed a DB question-

naire; they are called "questionnaire informants"; others were consulted by DB to confirm or clarify selected points; they are called "supplemental informants."

The number of informants on each topic in a country is small. For its 2007 report, DB received, on average, between one and four completed questionnaires per topic and consulted with up to three supplemental informants per topic for the 5 focus indicators in the 13 randomly selected countries of this evaluation, as summarized in table 2.1.[2]

Number of informants for each topic in a country is small.

The *starting a business* indicator has the most informants in each country—3.5 on average—perhaps because it has been used since 2004 and the questionnaire is relatively simple. But for the *paying taxes* indicator, there is a single survey informant in 142 countries—the local or regional office of the global accounting firm

Table 2.1: Average Number of Completed Questionnaires per Indicator in Each Country Is Low

| | DB dimensions | | | | | |
| | | | Getting credit | | | |
	Employing workers	Enforcing contracts	Legal rights	Private/public credit bureau	Paying taxes	Starting a business
Average number of questionnaire informants	1.7	1.8	1.5	1.5	1.0	3.5
Average number of supplemental informants per country	0.2	1.3	0.6	0.0	3.0	1.5

Note: Averages are calculated by dividing total informants by 13 countries, except for *getting credit* - public/private credit bureau, which includes 10 countries because Albania, Moldova, and Tanzania do not have credit bureaus.

PricewaterhouseCoopers LLC (PwC), with several people from each office contributing to one questionnaire for each country. This is because DB has established a partnership with PwC's global tax practice (described in chapter 3), in which PwC is the sole informant on the *paying taxes* indicator (except in the 33 countries where PwC does not participate at all). The information for the *enforcing contracts* and *employing workers* indicators is also based on not more than 2 completed questionnaires in each of the 13 countries.

Where information is factual, the small number of informants may not matter, but subindicators on time and costs include informed estimates.

To the extent that DB collects factual information, as distinct from opinion or perception, it arguably does not need a large number of informants to lessen the source of error, as do perception or opinion surveys. But, as will be noted in chapter 3, not all of DB's information is purely factual. The time and cost subindicators, for instance, require informants to make estimates based on their experience. Increasing the number of informants would reduce both the risk of erroneous factual information from a single informant and the errors inherent in questions requiring informants' judgments. An additional potential risk noted by some Bank Group staff is that interested parties could seek to influence informants' responses to improve their country's ranking. There is no evaluative evidence suggesting deliberate manipulation of data, but close relationships among lawyers and officials, especially in smaller countries, could

There are no clear selection criteria for informants.

impair informants' objectivity. Informants in Madagascar, for instance, are routinely in direct contact with the government department responsible for enhancing the investment climate. A larger number of informants would dilute the influence of any self-interested responses.

DB actively seeks new informants through referrals from existing informants, IFC and Bank contacts in borrowing countries, and local business directories. The DB Web site now invites prospective informants to register their interest in becoming data contributors. But there are no clearly stated criteria or processes for seeking and selecting informants.[3] To ensure that these efforts pay off in progressively more reliable data, DB should consider: (a) targeting them to the countries and indicators most needing increased reliability and (b) establishing selection criteria and numerical goals for new informants. It should report systematically on these activities.

Qualifications and Motivations of Informants

More than two-thirds of DB informants in the 13 countries reviewed by this evaluation are lawyers from private firms, as shown in figure 2.1. Eight percent are accountants, most from PwC accountancy offices.[4]

Informants interviewed for the evaluation were professionally engaged on the topic on which they provided information.[5] The DB team has noted that in small and/or low-income countries,

Figure 2.1: The Majority of DB Informants Are Lawyers and Accountants

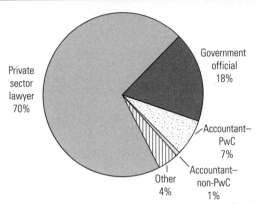

Note: Based on 141 questionnaire and supplemental informants. "Other" includes members of the private sector and one administrative staff member and graduate student in China.

it sometimes must rely on lawyers in general practice because there are no lawyers with specialized practices in bankruptcy, civil claims, or other relevant areas. In Burundi, for example, one informant was primarily a criminal and family lawyer with minimal experience in corporate law, and some informants for *closing a business* were unaware of the country's bankruptcy law. DB could reduce the risk of error through consulting in advance with Bank and IFC country counterparts in identifying informants and by undertaking greater quality assurance in coun-

tries with few specialized informants or a weak informant base. DB should also consider developing a systematic procedure or set of criteria for assessing informants' qualifications.

Generally, informants in the case study countries were professionally engaged on the topic they addressed.

DB does not pay its informants. It simply acknowledges the participating individuals in its publications (except for the approximately 10 percent who do not wish to be publicly named).[6] Assisting DB can require considerable effort; informants interviewed for the evaluation said they spent between one hour and one month on the exercise. The *paying taxes* and *getting credit* indicators are the most demanding of informants' time.

Why, then, do the informants participate? About half of those interviewed for the evaluation, as shown in figure 2.2, said participation would enhance their firm's credibility or prestige (46 percent). Another third said they wanted to share their experience (33 percent), and the rest said they were interested in the intellectual exercise, had free time, or were asked to participate by somebody else. Several lawyers mentioned they had gained clients who heard of them through the questionnaire, although attracting clients was not their objective in participating. In some Organisation for Economic Co-operation and Development (OECD) countries, lawyers noted that the time spent on DB counts toward the firm's commitment to provide *pro bono* services.

Informants generally participate for prestige or to share experience.

Figure 2.2: Why Do You Participate? For Prestige and to Share Expertise

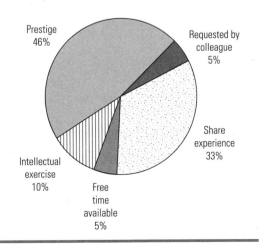

Not all those invited to participate actually do so; some decline, others agree but fail to follow through. DB does not keep track of nonparticipants and why they do not participate. If nonparticipants are systematically different from the actual informants, there is a possible selection bias, whose direction depends on the reasons for participation. For example, if informants are more likely than nonparticipants to be concerned about excessive business regulation in their country, the data may overstate the regulatory burden. If nonparticipants from small firms tend to decline because they lack junior staff to help complete a complex questionnaire, the data may understate the regulatory burden, because the informants will tend to be those with more capacity to help clients navigate the bureaucracy. Finally, if nonparticipants tend to be those too busy to do *pro bono* work, while informants are those with a lighter workload, the responses may be less reliable to the extent that the informants are those less well established in their field.

DB does not keep track of those who are invited to participate but do not, which makes it difficult to identify and disclose the nature and direction of participant biases.

Like most surveys and polls, DB involves participant bias, and it needs to systematically learn and disclose more about the magnitude and directions of nonresponse. In this regard, it may be useful to systematically collect and track information on the number of informants who were contacted, but who did not qualify as informants, were not interested in participating, or refused to participate for other reasons. DB should also consider diversifying its informant base to include business consulting firms, associations, and think tanks that meet the selection criteria to be developed.

Validating the Data

The DB team validates and adjusts the data based on documents and supplemental informants, but this makes it difficult to verify the data.

Once the informants' questionnaires are received, the DB team validates the information based on documents and consultations with supplemental informants. Typically there are four rounds of interaction between the DB team and the informants, involving conference calls, written correspondence, and in some cases a country visit. When informants' estimates of time differ, DB states that it selects the median value (World Bank-IFC 2006b, p. 61).

Country stakeholders and Bank Group staff in 6 out of 13 countries reported dissatisfaction with DB's process for validating data.

The evaluation reviewed the differences between the information provided in the completed questionnaires and the data points as reported.[7] For *employing workers* and *getting credit,* in all seven case study countries, *Doing Business 2007* published values that differed from at least one questionnaire, based on further consultation by the DB staff

with the informants and/or review of legislation. In the case of time estimates for *enforcing contracts,* the median value did not appear to have been selected.[8] Informants in Nigeria gave broad estimates of time, so DB staff calculated it based on a review of the current changes in legislation. In Mongolia, one informant's response was discarded in favor of another that reported no change since last year. Cost indicators may also require DB to select from different estimates. *Doing Business 2007* stated that in Spain, enforcing a contract cost 15.7 percent of the disputed debt, while the two informants had estimated 15.1 percent and 18.9 percent. DB explained that the higher estimate was disregarded because it came from a large international law firm. The estimate has subsequently been revised to 17.2 percent, close to the median of the two original responses.

DB's close attention to individual data points and its resolution of differences and anomalies undoubtedly help improve the quality of the database. The process also helps identify and weed out any unreliable informants. The DB team's organization along topic lines permits staff to develop a feel for plausible levels and ranges of the indicator values. At the same time, a risk is created by the considerable reliance placed on the decisions of DB staff to accept, overrule, or select among informants' replies, because this makes it difficult to verify or replicate the data. This risk is partly mitigated by a validation process in which DB sends proposed country data to relevant Bank and IFC staff and to country authorities (through their executive directors) for comment.

Bank Group staff and in-country stakeholders in 6 of the 13 countries reported dissatisfaction with the DB's process for validating the data.[9] Albanian officials, for instance, considered that the rankings for *starting a business, enforcing contracts,* and *protecting investors* do not square with the facts on the ground and found the response of the DB team to their rebuttals "not satisfactory." DB received 115 specific challenges and clarifications to its 2007 report from 50 country teams; 21 percent of these challenges were accepted.[10] Some Bank Group staff noted that despite recent improvements, DB still gives them insufficient time (just a few days in some cases) to review draft DB data. Some interviewees considered that their team's challenges were rejected by DB without due consideration. DB should consider how to devise a more open and in-depth validation process to help increase both the quality and the credibility of the data.

Publishing and Revising the Data

DB publishes its data and country rankings in its annual report each autumn and on its Web site. It makes ongoing changes to previously published data, and the Web site indicates that it contains the most current version. The DB 2007 data presented on the Web site in October 2007 had 2,284[11] differences (on the total 5,600 data points used to calculate the EODB ranking) from the data originally published in the DB 2007 report (see appendix C). The Web site does not provide nor link to the original data set. In the DB 2008 report, the revised 2007 data were used as the comparator for the previous year.

The DB 2008 report (World Bank-IFC 2007b, pp. 67–69) notes that data changes have been made and gives three reasons:

- Changes in methodology for three indicators: *enforcing contracts, dealing with licenses,* and *employing workers.* (Separately, the report indicates that the methodology for *paying taxes* was also changed [World Bank-IFC 2007b, pp. 78–79].)
- Corrections in 47 data points.
- Addition of three new countries.

The evaluation team's review of the changes to the DB 2007 data found that:

- Changes in methodology for the four indicators account for 1,284 changes in the DB 2007 data (56 percent of total changes). DB has not indicated how the 2008 methodology was retroactively applied to information that informants supplied in prior years on the basis of different assumptions or definitions. The DB team has ex-

plained that for three of these indicators (*paying taxes, enforcing contracts,* and *dealing with licenses*), some of the changes may also reflect data corrections, but that "it is difficult to separate corrected errors from methodology revisions."[12]

- Corrections account for 1,000 changes in the DB 2007 data (44 percent of total changes). The DB team has not indicated the reasons why information supplied by informants in prior years is subject to retroactive correction. The DB team has explained that "minor" changes to data for the prior year—that is, changes amounting to 10 percent or less of the original value—are made without further investigation. Of the 1,000 corrections, 222 (22 percent) were "minor."[13]

DB regularly revises previously published data . . .

- The addition of three new countries affected the rankings but not the underlying data being discussed here.

The practice of changing previously published data can be helpful in improving the reliability and consistency of a data set. At the same time, to fulfill its objective of facilitating research and informing theory, DB should disclose all such corrections and changes and explain their effects on the rankings as explained below, and make available previously published data sets.[14]

. . . but does not make available previously published data sets.

Effects of data changes on country rankings and top reformers

The DB Web site presents 2007 EODB rankings and a top reformers list derived from the revised data. It does not state how the changes in data affected these rankings. The evaluation finds that the 2,284 changes resulted in changes to the rankings for 106 countries (even after accounting for the addition of three new countries in 2008).[15] Twenty-four countries improved 10 or more positions and another 24 dropped 10 or more positions on the EODB ranking. The most significant changes are listed in table 2.2. The roster of top reformers also changed. Latvia entered by moving up from eleventh to tenth, and Ghana exited by falling from ninth to nineteenth.

Some data changes have had significant impact on ratings.

Table 2.2: Large Changes in 2007 Rankings Resulting from Data Revisions

	Five biggest winners				Five biggest losers		
Country	EODB October 2007	EODB August 2007	Change	Country	EODB October 2007	EODB August 2007	Change
Guyana	96	136	+40	Nicaragua	85	67	−18
Italy	49	82	+33	Samoa	59	41	−18
Turkey	64	91	+27	Tajikistan	151	133	−18
St. Kitts & Nevis	61	85	+24	Papua New Guinea	79	57	−22
Bhutan	120	138	+18	Uruguay	87	64	−23

DB should fully explain the nature and extent of periodic data changes and their implications for the rankings.

Some data changes nullify reforms cited in the text of the DB 2007 report. For example, 23 countries earlier identified as having reduced their corporate taxes show no changes in tax rates using the revised data. DB highlights reforms to *getting credit* in Italy and *trading across borders* in China, but the revised data revealed that the relevant subindicators actually deteriorated (World Bank-IFC 2006b, pp. 3, 30). DB should make clear that its rankings are subject to change and fully explain the extent, nature, and implications of these changes on country rankings.

Constructing the Rankings

The DB process first establishes cardinal values for each subindicator: time, costs, number of procedures, and the like. Countries are ranked on each subindicator. The subindicator percentiles are averaged to come up with an indicator-level ranking. The 10 indicator percentiles are then averaged to generate the overall EODB ranking.

The EODB is an average of 10 rankings.

DB's reliance on successive stages of ordinal rankings obscures the underlying cardinal values. The magnitude of the difference between the countries is not the same on all points of the distribution. For example, on total tax rate, there is a 5.1 percentage point difference between the top two performers, Maldives and Vanuatu, and a 4.7 percentage point difference between the bottom two, Gambia and Burundi. But the countries

A country's location in the distribution affects how a given reform will change its ranking . . .

ranked fifty-ninth and sixtieth (Israel and Mozambique) are separated by just 0.1 of a percentage point.

A given change in a cardinal value (for example, a reduction in the number of days needed for a procedure) is more likely to advance a country's rank, holding other countries' actions constant, if the country starts from a more concentrated segment of the distribution than if it starts from a more dispersed section. This arithmetic means that countries at the more dispersed parts of the distribution have to work harder to change their overall ranking. Countries can make significant changes, yet fail to improve their rankings, if they are at the dispersed sections of the distribution for that indicator. The following three examples illustrate this asymmetry by simulating the change in rankings for a subindicator, holding the actions of the other countries constant (see appendix B).

- *How does reducing the minimum capital requirement affect ranking on starting a business?* The DB 2008 report notes that Egypt drastically reduced its minimum capital requirement from 695 percent of income per capita to just 13 percent. Holding other countries' actions constant, this reduction would have boosted its ranking by 33 positions.[16] Although Gambia, Macedonia, and Saint Kitts and Nevis all reduced the minimum capital requirement much less than Egypt in absolute terms, they would have boosted their simulated rankings much more than Egypt. By eliminating the minimum capital requirement, these

3 countries would tie with the 66 others for first place on this subindicator.

- *How much does the tax rate have to fall to improve ranking on paying taxes?* With a 43 percentage point reduction in its total tax rate, Sierra Leone would improve only one position in the simulated ranking for *paying taxes.* But Latvia, by reducing the total tax rate by just 10 percentage points, could improve 17 positions because it is situated in the most concentrated segment of the distribution.

- *How does reducing the time to open a business improve starting a business? Doing Business 2008* notes that the Republic of Lao reduced the time to start a business by 60 days (36 percent of its starting value). Yet this change would not affect its simulated ranking for *starting a business.* Mauritius, by contrast, reduced the time by 41 days (89 percent of its starting value), and would thereby advance 20 positions on the simulated ranking for *starting a business.*

It has been suggested that DB's use of rankings might create an incentive for a country to reform the areas where it can most improve its ranking for the least reform effort. If this were the case, one would expect the highly concentrated subindicators to be associated with more reforms.[17] But the correlation between tightness of distribution and frequency of reforms is almost nonexistent (0.01).[18] The total tax rate is the third most frequent area of reform, and it has the tightest distribution of all the subindicators, with 94 percent of the countries' rankings within one standard deviation from the mean. But the two most popular areas for reform—number of procedures to start a business and legal rights of creditors and debtors—are not among the most tightly distributed. This quantitative analysis is fully consistent with the finding reported in chapter 4—that IEG did not find evidence of countries making superficial changes for the sole purpose of improving their rankings. Nevertheless, the DB team may wish to consider ways of making the rankings more informative, perhaps by establishing country groupings that reflect the cardinal values of each indicator.

. . . but IEG did not find evidence that countries use this characteristic of the ranking system to manipulate their DB indicator ranking.

Chapter 3

Evaluation Highlights

- For the most part, the indicators measure legal regulations and informed estimates of practice, as distinct from opinion.
- There are some systematic differences in rankings associated with countries' legal origins and policy choices; these do not undermine DB's validity.
- Inaccurate nomenclature and overstated claims of the indicators' explanatory power have provoked criticism.
- The subindicator on total tax rate is anomalous because it goes beyond regulatory burden.
- The *employing workers* indicator is consistent with relevant ILO conventions, even though it gives higher scores to countries with lower job protections.

Merchant buying oranges for his fruit stall, Epping Market, Cape Town, South Africa. Photo reproduced by permission of Gideon Mendel/Corbis.

What Do the Indicators Measure?

This chapter reviews key characteristics of the DB indicators as a group, and then focuses on issues that emerge from five indicators—*starting a business, paying taxes, employing workers, enforcing contracts,* and *getting credit.*

General Characteristics of the Indicators

Is DB rules-based?

DB states that it differs from other surveys because it collects information about a country's laws and regulations, as distinct from people's views, estimates, or perceptions.[1] The evaluation team analyzed the questionnaires for the 2007 and 2008 DB reports to determine the share of questions that required responses based:

- Solely on written laws or regulations
- On a combination of written law and the informant's experience
- Solely on the informant's judgment or experience.

The 2008 questionnaires contain 87 questions that generate data used to calculate the rankings for the 10 indicators and the aggregate EODB. Of these, 70 questions (80 percent) ask solely about the law as written.[2] For example, for *getting credit,* a question about the strength of legal rights index asks whether management is allowed to remain in control of a company during reorganization.[3] The remaining 17 questions on time and cost in the 2008 question-naires require a response that combines the law as written with an estimate of what happens in practice.[4] For example, on *enforcing contracts,* informants are asked the cost of resolving a commercial dispute, including both court fees and estimated average attorney fees.[5]

The 2008 questionnaires contain an additional 188 questions (109 additional questions in 2007) that are not used in the calculation of ratings or rankings. The responses are used to provide ideas for future work and additional insights into country issues. Of the 188 supplemental questions in 2008, 77 ask solely about the law, 67 ask about a combination of law and practice, and 44 ask for the informant's judgment or opinion. For example, the legal rights index questionnaire for the *getting credit* indicator asks informants' opinions about the main areas that require reform.[6] For *starting a business,* it seeks informants' opinions about how the registration process has changed since the previous year, as well as their suggestions for reforms.[7]

Thus, while DB's ratings and rankings are grounded predominantly in *Ratings and rankings are grounded in written laws and estimates of practice; opinions are collected but do not feature in the rankings.*

formal rules and regulations, DB also gathers informants' opinions or perceptions through these supplementary questions. The practice of asking extra questions adds to the complexity of the questionnaire, which may be a deterrent for potential contributors.[8] It may also give informants and readers the impression that DB rankings are based more on opinions than they actually are.

Nomenclature

The names of several indicators overstate what they actually measure.

The names of some indicators—getting credit, dealing with licenses, and employing workers—overstate what they measure.

- **Getting credit** does not measure firms' access to credit, which depends largely on macroeconomic and structural factors such as depth of financial intermediation and interest rates. It simply measures the availability of credit history information to lenders and the legal rights of lenders and borrowers should there be a default on the repayment of a loan.
- **Dealing with licenses** measures the ease of obtaining a construction permit, and not the wide range of licenses, permits, and authorizations required in all sectors for a wide variety of reasons.
- **Employing workers** measures the rules governing hiring, firing, and paying workers, but not other aspects of the labor market such as wages, mobility, and qualifications.
- **Registering property** measures the procedures to transfer the property title of land and a building between two businesses, and not the procedures to obtain a title for the property the first time.

Such broadly framed names might be justified if the indicators were proxies for broad but difficult-to-measure phenomena; DB has not systematically demonstrated that this is the case. Interviews with operational staff and stakeholders confirm that the simplicity of the names is helpful in getting the attention of ministers and other nonspecialist audiences. But even though DB's documentation makes amply clear what DB actually measures, country authorities, Bank Group staff, and other stakeholders have also criticized the DB for promising more explanatory power than it delivers. For instance, a donor

official noted, "*dealing with licenses* has been problematic because it has a broad name for what is a very narrow focus on construction permits and thus may be misleading." Bank staff and others who interpret the rankings to country authorities have urged DB to give a more accurate signal of what it measures. More precise nomenclature could help.

Legal origin

DB's 2004 inaugural report asserted that countries' regulatory regimes are strongly determined by their legal origin, as noted in box 3.1. This assertion, especially DB's contrast of the common and civil law systems, has spawned a debate on DB's treatment of countries with a civil law tradition, specifically of French legal origin.

Among the 175 economies covered by DB 2007, 76 trace their laws governing commerce and property to the Napoleonic Code, while 59 have a system based in common law.[9] Consistent with the assertion in *Doing Business 2004*, countries with a common law tradition occupy 8 of the top 10 spots for EODB. Of the 44 countries in the top quartile, 19 are common law and 14 are civil law countries. In the bottom quartile, 30 countries have a civil law origin, and these include all 17 members of Organization for the Harmonization of Business Law in Africa (OHADA).[10]

Box 3.1: Civil and Common Law Approaches to Regulation

The inaugural *Doing Business* report stated, "When the English, French, Spaniards, Dutch, Germans and Portuguese colonized much of the world, they brought with them their laws and institutions. After independence, many countries revised legislation, but in only a few cases have they strayed far from the original. These channels of transplantation bring about systematic variations in regulation that are not a consequence of either domestic policy choice or the pressures toward regulatory efficiency. Common law countries regulate the least. Countries in the French civil law tradition the most."

Source: Doing Business 2004, p. xiv.

The evaluation analyzed the specific issues on which the civil law countries as a group score lower than common law countries.[11] On 13 subindicators listed on the left in table 3.1, civil law countries scored significantly lower. Six of these significant differences relate to the number of procedural steps, commonly regarded as excessive in the French system. Four differences relate to the greater protection of debtors and the lesser protection of minority investors that characterize the civil law;[12] the DB indexes award points for attributes found primarily in common law.[13] Three differences relate to job protection, which may derive not from legal origin, but rather from policy choices made by this set of countries (see appendix D).

Even though some aspects of the civil law system are ranked lower on the DB indicator criteria, civil law countries can still score well on the DB indicators, as outlined in box 3.2.

Are the DB indicators adding new information?

A cross-country indicator whose rankings were perfectly correlated with per capita income (or some other underlying characteristic) would not add new information; one could predict a country's ranking by knowing its per capita income. For DB indicators, per capita income levels only partly explain the rankings. The overall EODB ranking and income per capita have a relatively high rank correlation coefficient of 0.77.[14] There is lower correlation (0.65) with per capita income in the low- and middle-income countries.[15] As shown in figure 3.1, countries with similar levels of gross national income (GNI) per capita, such as Peru and Brazil or Kenya and Mauritania, can have very different regulatory environments as measured by the DB indicators. Indeed, the rank correlation between DB indicators and GNI per capita is highest, at 0.89, for

On 13 of 32 subindicators, civil law countries score significantly lower than common law countries . . .

. . . nonetheless, civil law countries can still score well on the DB indicators.

Table 3.1: Do Civil Law Countries Score Lower Than Common Law Countries?

Differences are significant		Differences are not significant	
Indicator	**Subindicator**	**Indicator**	**Subindicator**
Highly significant[a]		Dealing with licenses	Procedures (number)
Employing workers	Difficulty of hiring index	Dealing with licenses	Cost (% of income per capita)
Employing workers	Rigidity of hours index	Employing workers	Firing costs (weeks of wages)
Employing workers	Difficulty of firing index	Registering property	Procedures (number)
Getting credit	Credit information index[b]	Registering property	Time (days)
Getting credit	Legal rights index	Registering property	Cost (% of property value)
Protecting investors	Director liability index	Protecting investors	Disclosure Index
Protecting investors	Shareholder suits index	Paying taxes	Total tax rate (% profit)
Starting a business	Procedures (number)	Trading across borders	Documents for export (number)
Starting a business	Cost (% of income per capita)	Trading across borders	Time for export (days)
Starting a business	Min. capital (% of income per capita)	Trading across borders	Cost to export (US$ per container)
Paying taxes	Time (hours)	Trading across borders	Documents for import (number)
		Trading across borders	Time for import (days)
Significant[a]		Trading across borders	Cost to import (US$ per container)
Paying taxes	Payments (number)	Enforcing contracts	Procedures (number)
Starting a business	Time (days)	Enforcing contracts	Time (days)
Dealing with licenses	Time (days)	Enforcing contracts	Cost (% of debt)
		Closing a business	Recovery rate (cents on the dollar)

a. Significance level set at 95 percent. Highly significant differences set at 99 percent.
b. All statistically significant differences favor English common law countries except for the credit information index.

Box 3.2: Can a Civil Law Country Succeed in a "Doing Business" World?

Having a civil law regime does not prevent a country from scoring well on the DB rankings. France, for example, ranks twelfth in *starting a business;* it has fast and inexpensive processes and no minimum capital requirement. It also ranks fourteenth in *enforcing contracts.* Countries can improve their scores and rankings within a civil law framework. Take, for example, Tunisia, a middle-income civil law country ranked eighty-eighth on EODB:

- If it improved its score on difficulty of firing to the same level as Belgium, it could improve its EODB ranking by 16 positions.
- Opening a business in Tunisia is fairly efficient in time and cost. If Tunisia eliminated the minimum capital requirement, like France, it would further improve its EODB ranking by 11 positions.

Even countries at the bottom of the rankings can improve. Of the 26 Sub-Saharan countries with a civil law tradition, 24 are in the bottom quartile of the overall ranking. Mali, ranked one-hundred and fifty-eighth in EODB, could improve substantially by following the model of Morocco or Tunisia. For example, if Mali reduced the number of procedures, days, and minimum capital requirement to start a business to the level of Morocco, it would improve 13 positions in the overall ranking. Likewise, improving the procedures for *enforcing contracts* and *trading across borders* to the level of Tunisia would improve Mali's overall ranking by 26 positions, allowing it to move out of the bottom quartile.

If a hypothetical civil law economy were constructed combining the scores of the highest-scoring civil law country on each indicator, it would place third in the overall ranking.

Note: Calculations based on the *Doing Business 2008* data.

Per capita incomes only partly explain the DB indicator rankings.

the richest and poorest countries[16]; for countries in the middle, it is 0.52. Many Bank Group clients thus have scope to reduce the burden of business regulations even at their current income levels.

DB includes 32 subindicators, as detailed in chapter 1. The rank correlation among them is generally low, suggesting that they are capturing different dimensions of the regulatory environment. [17] Out of a possible 509 pair-wise correla-

Figure 3.1: Countries with Similar GNI Can Have Different DB Indicator Scores

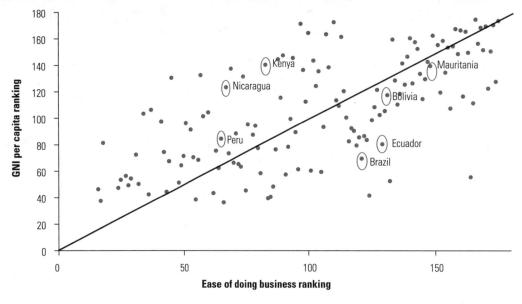

Sources: Doing Business 2007 and DB Web site.

tions, only 6 have correlation coefficients above 0.60, and 16 are between 0.5 and 0.6. Only the subindicators of the *trading across borders* indicator (DB's most recently added indicator) are so highly correlated with each other as to suggest that some may be redundant. For example, time to import and time to export have a correlation of 0.91. The DB team could consider dropping any such overlapping subindicators.

Key Features of Selected Indicators

The evaluation took an in-depth look at five DB indicators to identify what they really measure and to assess how the rankings track with reality in the case study countries.

Starting a business

Starting a business is one of the five original DB indicators and the first to have been developed by Djankov and others (2002).[18] It aims to measure how efficiently an entrepreneur can complete all officially required procedures to formally operate an industrial or commercial business. A country's ranking is the average of its percentile rankings on the four subindicators shown in table 3.2.

The underlying logic is that more onerous and costly entry regulations make opening a business more difficult, and thus fewer entrepreneurs will do so (at least in the formal sector). The DB reports note that "cumbersome entry procedures push entrepreneurs into the informal economy,

even after controlling for income per capita" (World Bank-IFC 2004, p. 22). DB states that informal businesses tend to lack worker protection and benefits, to have substandard product quality, and to face difficulty in securing bank credit and using courts to resolve disputes. Formalization is beneficial because "the establishment of a legal entity makes every business venture less risky and increases its longevity and its likelihood of success" (World Bank-IFC 2004, p. 17).

The time subindicator captures only the duration necessary to complete procedures; it excludes the time an entrepreneur may spend gathering information, which varies widely and cannot be reliably estimated with few data points. Opaque systems may require more time than transparent systems. Analysis using firm-level data suggests that this "time tax" may be large and important (Hellman and Schankerman 2000).

The logic behind the starting a business indicator is that more onerous and costly entry regulations result in fewer entrepreneurs opening businesses.

Doing Business 2004 asserts that just two procedures ought to be sufficient for regulating business start-up: the notification of existence and the tax and social security registration. While the report acknowledges that other procedures, such as registering with the statistical office, obtaining environmental permits, or registering workers for health benefits "seem to be socially desirable" (World Bank-IFC 2004, p. 21), DB

Table 3.2: The *Starting a Business* Indicator

Subindicator	Mean	Median	Min	Max	Standard deviation
Number of required pre- and post-incorporation procedures officially required to formally operate a business	9	9	2	20	3
Time to complete the procedures (calendar days)	44	31	2	694	61
Cost to comply with procedures (percentage of the country's income per capita)	61	21	0	1,075	122
Paid-in minimum capital that the entrepreneur must deposit in a bank before registration begins (percentage of the country's income per capita)	116	8	0	3,673	353

Source: Doing Business 2008.

awards higher ratings to countries without these procedures than to those with them (holding all other subindicators constant). At the extreme, the best performer for this subindicator would be a country that required just the above-mentioned two procedures, even though firms themselves may value the worker satisfaction or social benefits arising from other procedures.

Most popular indicator for reform

Since *Doing Business 2005*, the *starting a business* indicator has produced the most reforms annually as measured by DB. Reducing business entry regulations may be easier politically and less expensive than progress on other indicators, such as *employing workers,* that require political trade-offs. Further, since 2005, two subindicators—the days and cost of starting a business—have been used by the United States' Millennium Challenge Corporation (MCC) in its formula for determining countries' eligibility status for grants, and also features as a guidepost under the Bank's Country Performance and Institutional Assessment (CPIA) component on the "business regulatory environment." The time and cost to start a business are also used as 2 of the 14 "outcome" indicators in the "IDA results framework"[19] (see chapter 4).

The starting a business indicator has produced the most reforms as measured by DB.

One-stop shop: DB reports promote the creation of one-stop shops as a single access point for entrepreneurs to comply with entry regulations.[20] But a review of one-stop shops by the Foreign Investment Advisory Service (FIAS) finds that "such a mechanism works in barely any country of the world" (Sader 2002, p. 3). They tend to generate turf battles if a single agency gains control over all the various licenses, permits, and clearances formerly granted by different agencies. In this instance, DB's one-stop shop often becomes a "one-more-stop shop." The paper also notes that where one-stop shops have worked (such as in Ireland, Malaysia, and Singapore), the senior level of government had committed to investment climate reforms and made increased foreign

Literature is not conclusive about whether business registration reform encourages greater formalization and the creation of new formal businesses.

> **Box 3.3: A Paper "Reform" in Afghanistan**
>
> Afghanistan was the top reformer for *starting a business* in *Doing Business 2006* because it reduced the number of procedures from 28 to 1, and time from 90 to 7 days. Literature and key informants note that the authorities simply pushed all important procedures to a stage after the legal registration of a business.
>
> *Sources:* Arruñada 2007 and interviews.

direct investment (FDI) a central pillar of their development strategies. Thus, new one-stop agencies in these countries benefited from an environment where fewer licenses, approvals, and permits were deemed a necessary and important component of investment climate reforms.

Is it relevant and important for economic outcomes?

Doing Business 2007 claims two economic benefits of formally registered businesses: they grow larger and they pay taxes (World Bank-IFC 2006b). Literature and cross-country studies have established the importance of higher entry rates of new businesses for increased competition and economic growth (see, for example, Klapper, Laeven, and Rajan 2006). To what extent do registration procedures affect the entry of new businesses? After all, no matter how complicated and time-consuming they are, each business must endure them only once.

Cross-country studies have established a correlation between the number of small and medium-size enterprises or new firm registrations and less business entry regulation, but have not yet demonstrated causality (De Sa 2005, p. 4). For example, while Klapper and others (2007) find that barriers to starting a business are significantly and negatively correlated with the number of registered businesses and new registrations of companies, they acknowledge that they cannot postulate on the direction of causality.[21] Recent country-level studies have begun to address causality but depict a mixed picture. While in Russia and Brazil,[22] reform of specific regulatory procedures was linked to enhanced formaliza-

Box 3.4: Does Simplifying Business Registration Encourage Formalization?

Mexico implemented a program to simplify municipal licensing, one of several registration procedures for selected types of businesses. Firm registration increased between 4 and 5.6 percent in the eligible industries. Kaplan and others (2007) found that the increase was temporary and concentrated in the first 10 months after program implementation, leading the authors to conjecture that "the program mostly affects the existing stock of informal firms and has a smaller effect on the creation of 'truly' new firms" (pp. 4–5) as the program cleared a backlog of applications. Using household data, Bruhn (2007) found that while employment in eligible industries rose, the increase in firm registration comes "exclusively from former wage earners opening businesses" (p. 3). Rather than encouraging movement from the informal to the formal sector, registration benefited those already in the formal sector. [a]

Sources: Kaplan and others 2007; Bruhn 2007.

a. The authors conjectured that greater effects may have been seen if more comprehensive reforms had taken place.

tion and the creation of new businesses, respectively, two other studies in Mexico note the limited impact of business registration reforms, as illustrated in box 3.4.

Paying taxes

Paying taxes measures both the total taxes paid by a firm and the administrative efficiency of making the payments. A country's ranking is the average of its rankings on the three equally weighted subindicators, shown in table 3.3.

The lower the total taxes on firms, the higher a country scores on the total tax rate subindicator

(see box 3.5). This subindicator, unlike most other dimensions of DB, does not measure regulatory burden alone; it also involves implicit judgments on complex issues of fiscal efficiency and equity. The lower the taxes paid by the corporate sector, the more revenues need to be raised from other sources to reach a given revenue target. A country's preferred combination of corporate, sales, personal income, VAT, and trade taxes should represent a blend of revenue-generating capacity, efficiency, equity, transparency, and reasonable overall tax burden (IMF 2007). A lower tax rate on the corporate sector is not necessarily beneficial for the economy as a whole; assessments of tax regimes "need to be undertaken in an intertemporal, general equilibrium framework to capture the full impact of each choice" (OECD 2007a).

The total tax rate subindicator goes beyond regulatory efficiency to include judgment about fiscal policy.

DB's partnership with PricewaterhouseCoopers (PwC): The total tax paid, as measured by DB, includes not only corporate profit taxes, but also the social security and labor, property, capital gains, and dividend taxes that are paid by the firm. This comprehensive definition of taxes paid by the firm is based on a methodology initially devised by PwC, the global accounting partnership. PwC's objective in developing its "total tax contribution" framework was to persuade tax authorities—notably in the United Kingdom—that firms actually contribute more to the public coffers than is indicated by corporate tax rates alone.[23] DB adopted a version of PwC's methodology in 2005. (PwC 2007; World Bank-IFC 2007b, p. 77). The methodology is the most complex of all DB indicators, because it requires detailed calculations of a variety of taxes for a standard firm.

The methodology is based on a complex framework developed by PricewaterhouseCoopers.

Table 3.3: The *Paying Taxes* Indicator

Subindicator	Mean	Median	Min	Max	Standard deviation
Number of yearly payments	34	32	1	124	21
Time required (in calendar days)	323	242	0	2,600	322
Total tax rate as a share of firm profits	51	44	8	287	38

Source: Doing Business 2008.

Box 3.5: Can a Tax Haven Be a Global Leader on Taxation?

Kuwait, Maldives, United Arab Emirates (UAE), and Vanuatu are DB's four top-ranked countries on total tax rate in the 2008 report. Each has a special characteristic that enables it to avoid imposing taxes on firms. Vanuatu, a small Pacific island that has set itself up as a tax haven, does not impose personal or corporate income tax, capital gains tax, or withholding taxes. It raises revenues mostly from indirect sources, principally import duties and value added tax (VAT). Maldives also has no corporate income tax. Instead, the government raises revenues from tourism by charging lease rents on the land occupied by resorts. The government of Maldives is reviewing its dependence on these lease rents. Kuwait and UAE, for their part, derive most of their public revenues from oil and do not impose corporate, personal, or VAT taxes on domestic firms. These top-ranked countries cannot feasibly serve as role models for other countries seeking an optimal level of corporate taxation.

Sources: Heritage Foundation 2007; Maldives government 2007; Vanuatu government 2007.

The data for *paying taxes* are furnished to DB by PwC's partner offices in 142 countries.[24] This work is done under the terms of an agreement that PwC is DB's sole informant about taxes in all countries where it does business. PwC donates this work in return for the opportunity to co-publish the rankings jointly with DB, as part of its "thought leadership" activities.[25] This relationship offers DB the advantage of a ready-made stable of qualified informants. But DB's reliance on a single partner, combined with the complexity of the questionnaire, makes validation of information more difficult. Informants in Algeria, China, Mongolia, Netherlands, and Spain all noted errors in the tax data; thus reliability cannot be guaranteed.

The procedure for collecting complex data for the total tax rate subindicator entails two risks for DB: (a) the reputational risk arising from partnering

Table 3.4: The *Employing Workers* Indicator

Subindicator (lower score is always better)	Mean	Median	Min	Max	Standard deviation
Difficulty of hiring index (0–100)	32	33	0	100	27
Restriction on when term contracts can be used					
Maximum duration of term contracts					
Minimum wage (% of value added per worker)					
Rigidity of hours index (0–100)	39	40	0	80	23
Legal maximum of hours and days worked per week					
Restrictions on night and weekend work					
Paid vacation more than 3 weeks					
(score 1 for 22 days or more, 0 otherwise)					
Difficulty of firing index (0–100)	31	30	0	100	23
Steps required to fire 1 or a group of redundant					
workers – index contains 8 criteria dealing with					
required notifications and priority rules for redundancy					
Firing cost (weeks of salary)	48	35	0	446	50
Cost of advance notice required, severance payments,					
and penalties (score 0 if cost is 8 weeks' salary cost, or					
less; score number of weeks if more than 8 weeks salary)					
Nonwage labor cost[a]	15	14	0	55	11
Social security and similar payments (percent of salary)					

Source: Doing Business 2008.

a. Measured but not included in the calculation of rankings.

with an advocate of a particular policy stance, and (b) the operational risk of depending on a single source of data.[26] Since the subindicator itself is anomalous within the DB framework, it would be advisable for DB to reformulate the *paying taxes* indicator to include only measurements of regulatory burden such as the total cost of compliance. Since corporate tax rates are undeniably important for business, DB should continue to collect tax rate information separately and more simply, but exclude it from the rankings. This would also help to simplify the questionnaire, permit more informants to contribute, and make the data more understandable to users.

Employing workers

Employing workers rates the laws and regulations that govern how firms hire and fire workers: the length of the workday, week, and year and the minimum wage firms have to pay. The underlying assumption is that less regulation will result in higher employment rates and, in some contexts, lower shares of informal to formal employment.

A country's ranking on *employing workers* is the average of the percentile rankings on four equally weighted subindicators, listed in table 3.4. Firing workers is the focus of two of the subindicators, giving this dimension a 50 percent weight in the indicator. Three subindicators are indexes, each containing several criteria. With 15 criteria in all, *employing workers* is one of the more complex DB indicators.

The indicator and its components measure the costs of selected regulations but not their benefits. Since the stylized case involves a firm with 201

The reliance on a single global partner for the tax indicator makes validation difficult and cannot guarantee reliability.

The assumption underlying the employing workers indicator is that less regulation will result in higher rates of employment and more formal employment.

Table 3.5: *Employing Workers:* Highest- and Lowest-Ranked Countries

Top 20	DB 2008 rank	DB 2007 rank	Lowest 20	DB 2008 rank	DB 2007 rank
Singapore	1	1	Peru	159	160
United States	1	1	Senegal	160	163
Marshall Islands	1	1	Niger	161	161
Tonga	4	4	Mozambique	161	162
Brunei	4	n.a.	Gabon	163	166
Georgia	4	4	Luxembourg	164	n.a.
Maldives	7	7	Morocco	165	165
Australia	8	8	Slovenia	166	159
Palau	9	9	Congo, Rep.	167	167
Denmark	10	10	Ecuador	168	168
Uganda	11	11	Sierra Leone	169	169
Micronesia	12	12	Panama	170	170
New Zealand	13	13	Congo, Dem. Rep.	171	174
Bhutan	14	n.a.	Angola	172	171
Samoa	15	14	Paraguay	173	172
Fiji	16	15	Guinea-Bissau	174	173
Japan	17	20	Equatorial Guinea	175	175
St. Kitts and Nevis	18	16	São Tomé and Principe	176	176
Canada	19	17	Venezuela	177	177
Switzerland	20	39	Bolivia	177	178

Source: Doing Business 2008.

The indicator measures costs but not benefits of regulation or other dimensions of labor market flexibility.

Numerous small island states among the top 20 may reflect poorly developed labor legislation, yet they appear alongside countries with well-developed labor legislation.

unionized employees, it does not capture the laws and rules that affect smaller and nonunionized firms. Nor does it capture other dimensions of labor market flexibility, such as information, enforcement, and tied versus monetized benefits such as housing, pensions, worker health and safety regulations, and so on. *Employing workers* has been DB's most controversial indicator, perhaps because it delivers low rankings for some countries that have made policy choices favoring extensive job protection (see table 3.5).

The 20 lowest-ranked countries, displayed in the table, include Luxembourg, and France and Germany

also rank low at 144 and 137, respectively. As for the 20 highest-ranked countries, they include a surprising number of small island states—indeed, the Marshall Islands shares the top spot with Singapore and the United States. This may reflect the small islands' poorly developed labor legislation, as illustrated in box 3.6. Yet countries with well-developed labor legislation also appear in the top 20, including Australia, Canada, Denmark, Japan, and New Zealand. This reflects their mature public and private labor market institutions, which facilitate mobility with minimal regulation.

Eight countries are reported to have made positive reforms on *employing workers* overall in *Doing Business 2007*, making this the DB indicator with the fewest reforms (World Bank-IFC 2006b, p. 4; 2007b, p. 4). Georgia, though,

Box 3.6: Does Top-Ranked Imply "Well Regulated" . . . or "Unregulated"?

Because DB counts the number of regulations, it is difficult to tell whether top-ranked countries have efficient and responsible regulations or simply inadequate regulation. For example, on the *employing workers* indicator, Singapore and the Marshall Islands are both ranked number 1 (along with the United States), but their labor regulations are very different.

Singapore has strong labor regulations, effectively enforced	*Marshall Islands, a recent member of ILO, has important gaps in labor legislation*
The Right of Association	
Singapore's constitution provides all citizens the right to form associations, including trade unions. But the Parliament may impose restrictions based on security, public order, or morality grounds. In 2004, approximately 20 percent of the national labor force was represented by 68 unions.	The law provides for the right of free association in general, and the government interpreted this right as allowing the existence of labor unions, although none has been formed. With few major employers, there were few opportunities for workers to unionize, and the country has no history or culture of organized labor.
Prohibition of Forced or Compulsory Labor	
The law prohibits forced or compulsory labor, including by children, and there are no reports of such practices.	The law does not specifically prohibit forced and compulsory labor by children; however, there were no reports that such practices occurred.
Prohibition of Child Labor and Minimum Age for Employment	
The law prohibits the employment of children under the age of 12, and restrictions on employing children between ages 12 and 16 are rigorous and strictly enforced.	There is no law or regulation setting a minimum age for employment of children. Children typically were not employed in the wage economy, but some assisted in family enterprises.
Acceptable Conditions of Work	
The law sets the standard legal workweek at 44 hours and one rest day for each week.	There is no legislation on maximum hours of work or occupational safety and health.

Source: Bureau of Democracy, Human Rights, and Labor, U.S. State Department 2007 <http://www.state.gov/g/drl>.

improved dramatically from a rank of 71 to 6 as a result of a new labor code and flexible labor rules.[27] Reforms in this area are difficult because where organized labor is strong, they typically engage competing interests. Even where it is weak, as in many low-income countries, labor market reforms simply take low priority.

Is employing workers consistent with accepted labor standards?

Critics of DB have argued that the *employing workers* indicator rewards employment practices that are inimical to workers' interests (see, for example, Berg and Cazes 2007). They consider that regulations on job conditions, hiring, and firing are needed for the protection of workers. In response to these criticisms, DB has stated that the components of this indicator have recently been made consistent with the core labor standards of the International Labor Organization (ILO) (World Bank-IFC 2007a).

The evaluation examined this assertion and found it generally valid because:

- The ease of hiring index measures the ease and flexibility of using term contracts to employ workers. This issue is not covered by any ILO conventions.
- The rigidity in hours of work index consists of 5 components that are all consistent with the provisions of the ILO conventions.
- The firing cost and ease of firing index are based on responses to 10 questions, of which 6 are fully consistent with the respective ILO conventions, and 4 are consistent with the letter of the relevant ILO provisions, but not with their spirit, as shown in box 3.7.

This indicator is associated with the fewest reforms.

The ILO provisions, with which DB is consistent, represent a baseline degree of labor protection agreed to by the international community. Many countries' laws offer more extensive or generous job protections as a matter of national policy, and DB penalizes more generous provisions. For example, France and Germany, whose laws require 22 or more days of vacation, score worse on rigidity of hours than Australia or Italy, which require 21 days or fewer. This is what gives France, Greece, Spain, and

The employing workers indicator is consistent with the letter of ILO provisions, but four measures do not reflect their spirit.

Box 3.7: Measures on the Costs and Difficulty of Firing Workers and the ILO Conventions

There are four measures of DB's *employing workers* indicator that are consistent with the letter, but do not reflect the spirit, of the relevant ILO provisions:

Must the employer consider reassignment or retraining activities before redundancy termination? The ILO convention does not require, but asks the employer to provide, in accordance with national laws and practice, an opportunity for consultation with worker representatives about measures to mitigate the adverse effect of termination. DB gives a higher rating to countries that do not require the employer to make such consultations.

Are there clearly established criteria applying to redundancies? Although the ILO does not require application of clearly established criteria, it does recommend that employers select workers to be made redundant on that basis. The DB gives a higher rating to countries that do not require such criteria.

How much severance pay must a redundant worker get? The ILO stipulates that a redundant worker should be provided separation or severance pay based on seniority, wage level, and other unspecified criteria. DB sets its own cut-off, and in DB 2008, a country requiring up to eight weeks of severance pay gets the best score. All countries that require severance pay greater than eight weeks get the worst score.

Must the employer notify a third party before terminating a group of workers? ILO Convention 158 requires that the employer notify a competent authority about a termination of a group of workers. The convention does not specify the cut-off number or percentage of workers and leaves this to be determined in accordance with national laws and practice. Again, DB sets its own cut-off. In DB 2008, a country gets the worst score if it requires notification for terminating a group of fewer than 25 workers. In 2007, DB's cut-off was a group of 20 workers.

other European countries their low overall rankings on *employing workers*.

Enforcing contracts

The *enforcing contracts* indicator aims to measure how efficiently a commercial dispute can be resolved. The underlying logic is that a higher degree of contract enforceability encourages firms to develop relationships with a larger number of suppliers and customers, fostering profitability and incentives to engage with more advanced technologies (Commander and Tinn 2007). This indicator (like most DB indicators) is linear; that is, fewer procedures are always considered better. It does not consider that some judicial procedures may help ensure transparency, accountability, and fairness to the parties.

The enforcing contracts indicator considers that it is always better to have fewer procedures.

The informants—lawyers and notaries—base their answers on a scenario involving a seller of goods suing a buyer who does not pay for the goods, citing poor quality. The amount in dispute is 200 percent of the country's per capita GNI. The ranking on *enforcing contracts* is the average of the country rankings on the three subindicators, as shown in table 3.6.

The methodology for the enforcing contracts indicator changed substantially, resulting in large changes in rankings.

DB periodically changes the methodology for some indicators (for example, World Bank-IFC 2007b, p. 62), and the methodology for *enforcing contracts* has changed more than most. In the 2007 report, the scenario was changed from a bounced check to a commercial dispute,[28] which prevents the construction of a consistent time series for this indicator. Further changes were made for the 2008 report, and the 2007 ratings were retroactively revised.[29] These changes had a significant impact on the ratings and rankings. For example, Tunisia, praised in *Doing Business 2006* as one of the easiest places to enforce contracts (World Bank-IFC 2005, p. 61) and ranked fortieth in *Doing Business 2007*, now ranks a mediocre eightieth in *Doing Business 2008*. These changes were explained by changes to the methodology. Such large changes in the data from one year to the next make data on individual countries and the rankings less than fully reliable, as discussed in chapter 2.

Most disputes do not wind up in court

All the DB indicators attempt to measure the law as distinct from actual practice. In the case of *enforcing contracts*, the gap between law and practice is particularly wide. The indicator measures only contract enforcement through the court system, and not other formal and informal resolution methods commonly used in many countries. In practice, a lawyer will select the most cost-effective legal strategy to help a client recoup funds. The 2005 Business Enterprise Surveys (covering 38 countries) found that two-thirds of business owners said they had resolved their most recent dispute over the payment of an overdue bill without resorting to the courts. In the United States, only about 10 percent of the civil cases in state courts go to court (Davis and Kruse 2007), while in Romania, about one-third of such cases go to court.[30] The

Table 3.6: The *Enforcing Contracts* Indicator					
Subindicator	Mean	Median	Min	Max	Standard deviation
Number of required procedures between filing a suit and enforcement of judgment	38	38	20	55	7
Time taken to resolve the dispute (in calendar days)	605	543	120	1,800	308
Cost to defendant and plaintiff including attorney and court fees, expressed as a percentage of the claim value	34	26	0	163	28

Source: Doing Business 2008.

indicator, therefore, tends to overstate the burden of court procedures across the board, and disproportionately more in those countries where noncourt mechanisms are used the most. To partially correct this, the 2008 DB survey introduced a one-procedure "credit" to the score of countries with specialized commercial courts. This change reduced the counted number of procedures in 11 countries.

Stakeholders confirmed that DB data on contract enforcement diverge from practice. Moldova's high rank of 17 does not reflect the reality that few disputes wind up in court. Indeed, a Bank-supported analysis finds that the main reasons Moldovan businesses do not resort to courts are the long duration of the process for settling disputes and the high cost of legal services (World Bank 2007d, p. 68). In Peru, although specialized commercial courts have reduced the number of procedures and time needed to resolve a dispute, interviewees noted that the type of case specified under the DB methodology would not necessarily go to court.

Is it important for economic outcomes?

The DB 2006 and 2007 reports suggest that the ease of enforcing commercial disputes in courts is important because it is associated with higher lending from commercial banks, increases in the number of new firms and new hires in established firms, and reduced demands on court budgets. The underlying research, Djankov and others (2002), finds excessive formalism in judicial procedures in countries. Djankov and others (2006) construct a debt enforceability index that is found to be correlated with income per capita, credit market development, and legal origins.

A background paper commissioned for this evaluation found no significant association between the *enforcing contracts* indicator and a range of intermediate outcomes—research and development, investment, domestic credit, gross capital fixed formation, domestic bank credit, gross capital inflows, or foreign direct investment (see Commander and Tinn 2007). The analysis also found little association between the *enforc-*

ing contracts indicator and measures obtained from firm-level surveys on aspects of the legal systems for *enforcing contracts* and loans given with collateral.

While there may be some time lag between improvements in the DB indicator and outcome measures, the DB report needs to be cautious when making associations or implying causality between the *enforcing contracts* indicator and outcomes such as enhanced foreign direct investment (see World Bank-IFC 2006b, p. 48, for example).

Getting credit

The *getting credit* indicator measures two things: the legal rights of borrowers and lenders (strength of legal rights index) and the availability of credit information about firms and individuals (depth of credit information index). The strength of legal rights index measures how well collateral and bankruptcy laws facilitate lending. It assigns a country one point for each of seven attributes of collateral law and three of bankruptcy law, based on information provided by financial lawyers. Hong Kong and the United Kingdom have the highest score of 10, and Afghanistan and Cambodia have the lowest score of 0.

The depth of credit information index measures the quality, scope, and accessibility of credit information through public and private credit registries. The data are derived from banking supervision authorities and credit registries. The depth of credit information index assigns one point for each of six features of a credit information system. Twenty-one countries have the highest score of 6, and 56 countries have the lowest score of 0. The top 10 countries for *getting credit* are all high-income countries, except Malaysia and the Slovak Republic.

Additionally, DB gathers data on the share of the population covered by public credit registries

Stakeholders note that the scenario for this indicator diverges significantly from practice.

IEG analysis found no significant association between the enforcing contracts indicator and a range of intermediate outcomes.

The getting credit indicator measures borrower and lender legal rights and the availability of credit information.

Table 3.7: The *Getting Credit* Indicator

Subindicator	Mean	Median	Min	Max	Standard deviation
Strength of legal rights index (0–10)	5	4	0	10	2
Index contains 10 criteria dealing with collateral and bankruptcy laws to protect borrowers and lenders					
Depth of credit information index (0–6)	3	3	0	6	2
Index contains 6 criteria dealing with the scope, accessibility, and quality of information available through public or private credit registries					

Source: Doing Business 2008.

and private bureaus, but these data are not included in the calculation of the overall EODB ranking.

According to *Doing Business 2004*, two factors expand access to credit and improve its allocation: credit information registries and creditor rights in the country's secured-transactions and bankruptcy laws. Good credit institutions protect both creditors and debtors and make everyone better off. Because credit histories are available, borrowers benefit from lower interest rates, as banks compete for good clients.

There is research support for this argument. Love and Mylenko (2003) found that private credit registries are positively related to availability of bank financing for small and medium-size firms and that stronger rule of law is associated with more effective private credit registries. Nevertheless, they note that there is no evidence of causality between the creation of private registries and their effects on financing constraints. Jappelli and Pagano (2002) found that bank lending is higher and credit risk lower in countries where lenders share information, regardless of the private or public nature of the information-sharing mechanism. Dorbec (2006) concluded that credit information sharing between lenders increases the supply of financing, decreases defaults, and enhances monitoring of the risks taken by the financial system. A

The literature supports the argument that credit information registries and creditors' legal rights help expand access to credit.

background paper commissioned for this evaluation found better legal rights of borrowers and lenders to be positively associated with private credit, gross private capital flows, and net foreign direct investment (Commander and Tinn 2007).

A 2007 World Bank review of financing constraints suggests that information-sharing mechanisms matter most in low-income countries, while enforcement of creditor rights is more important in high-income countries (World Bank 2007a). Other nonprice factors include: more important limitations on access to credit, including geography (or lack of physical access); lack of proper customer documentation for identification, especially in low-income countries; and high minimum account balance requirements (World Bank 2007a).

In sum, the DB indicators are designed to measure dimensions of the regulatory environment that are indeed important, although not equally important in all countries. The total tax rate is anomalous, because although it is important to business owners, it does not measure regulatory burden like the rest of the DB indicators. For the most part, the indicators measure actual legal rules and regulations and informed estimates of practice, as distinct from opinion. Their relevance in a particular country setting depends on the extent to which the laws are applied, which DB does not measure. Although in many circumstances it is the law on the books that causes inefficient outcomes, understanding what actually happens on the ground is essential (La Porta and others 2007). The impact of a given reform will likewise vary across countries.

There are a few systematic differences in country rankings associated with legal origins. These are consistent with the ideas behind the DB framework and they have little impact on the overall rankings or the validity of the exercise. The *employing workers* indicator is consistent with relevant ILO conventions, but it does give higher scores to countries with lower job protections. Inaccurate nomenclature and overstated claims of the indicators' explanatory power provoke considerable criticism and should be rectified.

Chapter 4

Evaluation Highlights

- DB's simple and bold communication is integral to the product, but at times simplicity comes at the expense of rigor.
- DB has successfully spurred debate and motivated dialogue and additional analyses on regulatory burdens and investment climate issues in developing countries.
- As a cross-country benchmarking tool, the DB indicators cannot fully capture country-specific nuances and policy idiosyncrasies. Thus they have had less influence on designing reforms than on spurring debate.
- The DB indicators' utility for research could be enhanced by explaining the extent of data changes and making available previously published data sets.
- The DB indicators are an important addition to the Bank's knowledge toolkit: they introduced benchmarking based on actionable indicators.
- The DB indicators appropriately do not drive the Bank's operational or resource-allocation decisions.

Women pack table grapes for export, South Africa. Photo reproduced by permission of Kip Ross/National Geographic Image Collection.

Communicating and Using the Indicators

The DB indicators are designed to encourage policy makers to use them as an aid to decision making. Accordingly, DB makes communication and dissemination part and parcel of the core product. This chapter reviews how the DB indicator team communicates with audiences and how the DB indicators have been used in a variety of settings.

Presentation Style

DB reports are presented in commendably simple and straightforward terms. For example, "Egypt's reforms went deep" and "Thirty-nine countries made start-up simpler, faster or cheaper" (World Bank-IFC 2007b, pp. 2, 3). A Foreign Investment Advisory Service (FIAS) official said that countries become interested in the DB issues because "at last they can understand a Bank report. Everybody understands a ranking."[1] A former prime minister interviewed for the evaluation said: "The World Bank is in the stone age. The public relations techniques are primitive. But IFC [International Finance Corporation] has done well with DB." But the drive for simplicity sometimes results in inaccuracies or statements that are inadequately supported by evidence. For example:

- Simple causal relationships are asserted where the evidence supports only association and where the causal factors are complex. For example, *Doing Business 2008* states, "Countries that make it easier to pay taxes have lower rates of unemployment among women. The reason is simple: a burdensome tax system disproportionately hurts smaller businesses, especially in the services sector where most women work."[2] Intercountry differences in female unemployment rates actually reflect many social, macroeconomic, and business factors; the ease of paying corporate taxes plays only a small part. Another example: "Each additional day that an export product is delayed reduces exports by more than 1 percent" (World Bank-IFC 2007b, p. 44). No source is cited for this statement, which in any case should be expressed as an association, since there are many other variables that affect differences in export volumes.

The DB reports are admired for their simplicity, but this sometimes undermines rigor.

- The reports present information correlating performance on an indicator with broad economic outcomes such as increased foreign direct investment, although such links have not been fully documented in literature.

Lack of rigor in presenting information needlessly risks undermining DB's credibility. The DB data and messages can and should be presented readably without sacrificing rigor.

Communications Strategy

A media strategy of maintaining high visibility to promote debate and action is integral to DB.

Doing Business stands out among Bank Group products for the variety and innovativeness of the communications tools it uses, as illustrated in box 4.1. The aim of the media strategy is to promote action through increased public debate and competition among countries based on DB's annual benchmarking exercise. To achieve this, the primary effort of the communications strategy is simply to increase media coverage and maintain a high and visible international profile for the product.

The DB Web site is central to its communications efforts.

Three stages of communication activities carried out following each year's publication are:

- Global and Regional pre-launch and post-launch virtual press conferences
- Road shows involving media events and presentations to domestic policy makers and a diverse group of stakeholders (organized and sponsored in large part by Bank Group country offices)[3]
- Two-day workshops on DB findings and methodology and local media events in 40 countries.

Communications are primarily targeted to the 10 top reformers identified each year. In other countries, road shows are held on the basis of demand from Bank and IFC country offices. An additional key part of the communications strategy is the development and maintenance of an updated and interactive Web site. In fiscal 2007, the DB team reported spending approximately $1,000,000 for dissemination events led by DB team management and members, support from a communications team, and maintenance of the Web site.[4] Not included in these estimates are the time and costs incurred by country units in (a) reviewing the DB reports and providing comments, (b) explaining and addressing government comments on the DB data and methodology, and (c) technical assistance/training related to the DB indicators paid for by the country teams. The DB team receives revenue

The communications outputs are monitored, but not their influence on public opinion or policies.

from the sales of its reports, estimated at $100,000 per annum.

The DB team monitors and reports on a range of outputs from its communications program, including its press citations, media events, Web site hits, downloads, and citations. The research papers that are the basis for the DB indicators have been cited in 676 academic papers, according to DB's count (World Bank-IFC 2007a). In June 2007, the DB Web site was the World Bank Group's most visited online database, with over 120,000 hits. The results of this monitoring effort attest to DB indicators' high media coverage and public awareness. But the monitoring does not ascertain systematically what results are achieved in changed public opinion and/or country policies.

DB is effective in reaching audiences. Stakeholders in 6 of 12 countries mentioned the DB indicators unprompted when asked to recall economic and sector work that had been helpful or influential.[5] Bank Group staff noted that the DB indicators' extensive press coverage attracts the interest of senior policy makers, government officials, and the business community in its messages.

Box 4.1: Key Features of DB Communications

- Messages expressed in straightforward style
- Report translated into up to 5 other languages[a]
- High-quality Web site with interactive capabilities
- In-person and video presentations to country stakeholders and decision makers
- Road shows and media presentations hosted by Bank Group country offices
- Customized country reports
- Launches of spin-off publications, translations, and topical reports
- Innovative approaches using social media
- Active participation of product team in marketing and communication.

a. *Doing Business* has been translated into French, Spanish, and Portuguese (2005, 2006, and 2007); Russian (2004, 2005, and 2006); Arabic (2004 and 2005); and Chinese and German (2005).

How does this intensive dissemination translate into practical use? Six ways in which DB has been used are reviewed below, along with the strengths and risks of each.

A Tool for Regular Cross-Country Benchmarking

Stakeholders in all 13 countries reviewed[6] consider the chance to benchmark their country against neighbors, peers, or competitors to be a main motivator for dialogue about the business environment. Country policy makers and stakeholders use the DB indicators to compare aspects of their regulatory framework with those of neighboring or competitor countries and to diagnose their weaknesses. This was the most frequently and favorably cited use of DB indicators noted by the evaluation. Seventeen of 29 stakeholders (59 percent) interviewed in the 13 countries as well as 24 of 42 Bank Group staff (57 percent) interviewed ranked the DB indicators "very useful" in enabling cross-country benchmarking,[7] as box 4.2 illustrates.

Bank staff working in the Africa Region commented that the aggregate ranking may motivate governments to reform because they perceive it as a signaling device for potential investors, especially foreign investors. The risks of an overly simplistic connection between DB indicator ranking and foreign investment may be greater in countries with very limited capacity to undertake reform.

The DB provides countries with a cross-country benchmarking tool. Its comparative nature spurs policy debate.

Even stakeholders who found DB indicators useful for benchmarking questioned or criticized aspects of the methodology and process. Each year the DB team receives numerous queries and complaints from governments, both directly and channeled through Bank and IFC country staff, about the rankings and how they are calculated. "Often Country Management Units are called upon by counterparts (often very irate counterparts) to explain the basis of scores or ranking."[8] Apart from numerous challenges and debates about details of fact, country and Bank staff interviewees raised methodological concerns about some of the areas discussed in chapter 2. Stakeholders noted that:

Even stakeholders who find DB benchmarking useful question its methodology and process.

- Data informants are too few or represent prominent law and accounting firms that are more likely to have primarily large and/or foreign firms as clients.
- DB data is collected for the capital city and may not be valid for other parts of the country.

Box 4.2: Keeping up with the Neighbors: DB Indicators Foster Benchmarking

- Bank Group staff in Africa commented that DB indicators are very useful because they provide cross-country benchmarking data previously unavailable in many countries. Bank Group staff in Burundi noted that the DB indicators are the "only source out there" that allows for cross-country comparisons related to the business environment.

And elsewhere...

- By providing information about other countries, DB shows the potential for improving regulations and legislation. *(Vietnam government official)*
- The DB indicators help to raise greater awareness within the country on the need to improve our overall competitiveness. *(Tanzania government official)*

- Algerian policy makers monitor how Algeria fares compared to Morocco and Tunisia. *(Bank Group staff)*
- Ranking with peers provides incentives for reforms, not the survey itself. I see the value of DB indicators in Albania when we have policy dialogue and tell the authorities Serbia did better last year and jumped X steps in the ranking because they did X, Y, and Z. *(Bank Group staff)*
- DB was used by donors, Bank, and others to point out the deficiencies that the Investment Climate Assessment had pointed to earlier by benchmarking Mongolia against other countries. This really helped open the eyes of the government and Mongolians and galvanized them to take action. *(Bank Group staff)*

DB rankings need to be interpreted with care.

- The firms depicted in the hypothetical cases are larger than the typical firm in middle- and low-income countries, so the rankings may fail to pick up improvements to the business climate for micro and small enterprises.
- Changes in methodology, data, and rankings make it difficult to explain and interpret DB indicators to legislators and the public.
- DB indicators lack a systematic validation process that draws on the experience of country teams and country stakeholders.
- The indicators omit measures of important constraints on business, as discussed in chapter 3.

Clients' doubts about aspects of DB's methodology could, if not allayed, jeopardize the use and impact of the report, as audiences question the relevance to their country's reality. As an Albanian official expressed it, when there are as many disagreements on indicators and overall rankings as there are now, the report is seen as a "dismotivator" in international conferences on foreign direct investment. Bank Group staff observed that the Chinese authorities pay less attention to DB than to other cross-country benchmarks on rule of law, the investment environment, global competitiveness, trade and logistics, and corruption, because they consider China's poor DB rankings inconsistent with its strong private sector growth. More generally, stakeholders in all the case study countries noted that they find the general findings of the DB cross-country benchmarking useful, but do not always rely on the exact numbers.

DB has led to additional diagnostic work in Peru and Nigeria.

A Catalyst for Dialogue

In many countries, discussion around DB, even when contentious, has opened up a productive dialogue between policy makers and other stakeholders about the business climate. DB's active dissemination and simple communications style permits widespread press coverage, fostering interest from business and NGO communities, and attracting the attention of the most senior policy makers.

DB has successfully stimulated dialogue on business climate issues.

In both Moldova and the Netherlands, for instance, efforts to reduce the regulatory burden on business had begun before the advent of the DB indicators in 2003, but the DB indicators increased awareness of regulatory issues and increased the pressure for further reforms.

Rwanda's Economic and Finance Commission asked DB to explain its methodology after the country failed to make the top reformers list in the 2007 report. The presentation led to a workshop that involved over 70 participants including legislators, officials, business persons, and donors. The resulting task force remains under the aegis of the president's office.

Tanzania's multidonor Business Enterprise Strengthening in Tanzania (BEST) program to streamline licensing and registration procedures got off to a slow start. The Bank's involvement, along with the publication of the DB indicators, drew the attention of the president and other senior officials, helping Tanzania gain a top reformer spot in 2007.

DB has also inspired some countries to do additional diagnostic work. In Peru, *Doing Business 2006* drew the attention of Lima's mayor to the difficulties of starting a business in the capital. Drawing on diagnostic work by FIAS and technical assistance from the IFC, the municipality reformed the process for obtaining a business license. The reform template is now being promulgated by the National Council for the Simplification of Municipal Procedures for Businesses. In Nigeria, the United Kingdom's Department for International Development (DFID) is supporting the collection of DB indicators for every state. The data will be used for diagnostic analysis and as benchmarking by the government and donors.

A Guide to Policy Reform

While the vast majority (85 percent) of interviewees affirmed DB's usefulness for motivating reforms, less than half (44 percent) considered it helpful as a guide to action because it offers little guidance about the priorities, sequencing, and policy coherence needed to implement a successful reform program. Moldova's home-grown *Cost of Doing Business* assessment, which surveys perceptions of 600 small and medium-size enterprises, finds that businesses are most concerned about arbitrary interference from police and uniformed services in their daily operations—a topic outside DB's ambit. Bank Group staff working on China noted that a perception-based survey of businesses in 120 cities was helpful in highlighting the constraints faced by businesses and encouraged reform in a number of cities. A Bank Group staff member working on Albania stated, "We cannot build projects or TA [technical assistance] programs on the DB indicators. It is just indicative about the business climate and is used to provide incentive to countries to improve the business climate. Our counterparts understand the limitations of the methodology."

DB annually designates 10 countries as top reformers. The "Reformers Club" provides a forum for recognizing countries that have made the largest changes in ranking in a given year. These are countries that have both improved their rankings on at least three individual indicators—indicating "breadth of reform"—and improved the most on their overall EODB ranking from the previous year—indicating "depth of reform." This method rewards the quantity of rankings changes and does not attempt to assess whether the changes constitute important or meaningful reforms. While the approach is practical and transparent, as Hausmann, Rodrik, and Velasco (2005, pp. 5–6) note, "We cannot be assured that any given reform taken on its own can be guaranteed to be welfare promoting, in the presence of multitudes of economic distortions. . . . and welfare may not be increasing in the number of areas that are reformed." An alternative approach would be to design reforms to address the most "binding constraints" in order to produce the biggest bang for the reform buck (Hausmann, Rodrik, and Velasco 2005, p. 7). Because the DB indicators neither prioritize among the 10 dimensions nor provide detailed country-level analysis, they are not suited to designing reform programs targeted at critical bottlenecks.

DB's direct impact is thus difficult to determine and appears limited, even in countries designated as top reformers. For instance, in Tanzania, *Doing Business 2007* noted improvements in *trading across borders* because of modernization of customs procedures. Staff and stakeholders noted that while DB motivated authorities to look at the issue, the process of modernizing procedures relied heavily on other Bank diagnostics and the country's own detailed studies. To guide its business climate reforms, the Netherlands uses its indigenously developed Standard Cost Methodology, with an added emphasis on regulatory burdens that require the firm to undertake activities outside the scope of regular business operations. The DB indicators are seen as a useful tool for monitoring progress, but not a principal source for prioritization of government actions or policies.

Because the DB indicators cannot and do not capture country-specific policy nuances, they have had less influence in designing reforms.

DB identifies countries as reformers based on changes in country rankings, without regard to the relevance and quality of the reform . . .

As noted in chapter 3, since the DB indicators cannot capture country-specific policy nuances, they cannot and do not help counties to situate particular improvements within broader reform efforts nor ensure adequate sequencing and policy coherence, needed to implement and sustain the changes in legislation. For instance, in Algeria and Moldova, the governments experimented with the creation of one-stop shops for licensing, which in Algeria included construction permits and was counted by DB as a reform. But the pilot in Algeria is underutilized, and Moldovan ministries continued to require other forms of revenue-generating activities such as "authorizations" and "permits" before procuring a license. The one-stop shop simply added another regulatory layer.

. . . it is thus not suited to designing reform programs targeting critical bottlenecks.

An obstacle to using the DB indicators as a guide to action is that some indicators measure specialized aspects of a larger problem, as discussed in chapter 3. Many stakeholders mentioned that DB's *dealing with licenses* indicator, which

Some DB indicators measure specialized aspects of a larger problem.

relates to construction permits, has had limited usefulness in guiding the broad reforms of licensing. For example, Niger reduced the number of procedures measured by *dealing with licenses* from 27 to 19 by eliminating numerous security inspections at the construction site, but this reform is unlikely to result in real improvements to the licensing regime as a whole. Similarly, in Tanzania, Nigeria, and Rwanda, access to credit and cost of financing are important constraints not measured by DB's *getting credit* indicator; while the credit bureau information it does measure is not considered relevant by stakeholders in Rwanda.

Have countries tried to improve their ratings by changing the letter of the law without making serious reforms? Interviewees with Bank and IFC country teams, FIAS, and the Millennium Challenge Corporation (MCC) cited instances of country officials asking how to increase their DB rankings (India) or making the increase in DB rankings a goal in itself (Georgia and Madagascar). The ratings simulator in the DB Web site encourages users to see the effects of possible changes. And the DB team has provided country officials with suggestions of specific actions they could take to improve their indicators upon request. But none of the 13 countries reviewed by this evaluation took an unduly or cynically narrow approach or "easy" steps purely to affect the ratings. Even where officials initially aimed to reform only those aspects measured by DB, they were persuaded by Bank and IFC staff to take a comprehensive approach to business climate reforms. FIAS and MCC staff noted that they use such inquiries to open a dialogue on genuine reform options.[9] Often this involves detailed explanations by Bank staff and other donors to country counterparts about the methodology of DB and what each indicator measures.

IEG did not find evidence that countries took an unduly narrow approach solely to increase their rankings.

The FIAS Rapid Response Unit will need to ensure its advice is integrally aligned with the Bank Group's advice and recommendations.

FIAS has recently created a Doing Business Rapid Response Unit with a mandate to help countries adopt measures that are "strictly DB-related."[10] While this unit does aim to introduce and involve experts in the relevant areas from other parts of the Bank, it expects that "broader reform suggestions" will be managed by the other relevant units. To avoid an implied endorsement of quick fixes, the Rapid Response Unit will need to ensure its advice to a country is integrally aligned, and perceived by clients to be aligned, with the Bank Group's overall Private Sector Development (PSD) Assessment and other recommendations.

The DB indicators do not capture the extent to which changes in legislation or streamlining of procedures are actually implemented. There is no clear articulation of the impact of the DB-measured reforms on firm performance, perceptions of regulatory burden, or the overall regulatory environment in a country. In Vietnam, Bank Group staff reported using DB's *getting credit* indicator to open a dialogue with the Ministry of Justice on a plan for improving the collateral lending environment and to advocate for the creation of a private credit bureau in the State Bank of Vietnam. But both staff and an informed stakeholder noted that only a small number of individuals and businesses were using the collateral registry. It is not clear what the effects of the private credit bureau and collateral system have been.

A Research Tool

DB's near-universal country coverage, combined with the accessibility of the data and methodology notes on the Web site, make it a useful tool for analyzing regulatory issues. But yearly changes in methodology and retroactive changes to prior year data without making available previously published data sets makes it difficult for research to be validated and replicated. This disadvantage could be attenuated if the Web site fully disclosed and explained all corrections and changes and their effects on the rankings and provided previously published data sets.[11]

A second disadvantage is the small number of informants supplying the underlying data, as discussed in chapter 2. Given the very small number of completed questionnaires on each indicator in a given country, it is not possible to calculate meaningful standard errors or confidence intervals. DB needs to make transparent the number of completed questionnaires that form the basis for each indicator in a country.

A Criterion for Operational Decisions

The MCC uses two DB subindicators—days and cost to start a business—in its formula for selecting countries eligible for grants. Together, these subindicators account for 6 percent of a country's score. In 2008, MCC will add DB's subindicators of time and cost to register property, raising DB's weight to 9 percent. The DB indicators have, according to MCC officials, sparked more interest by ministers than most other parts of their scorecard because they are easy to understand and convey to the public and point to specific areas that may need improvement. On the down side, MCC officials noted that eligibility decisions had been made on the basis of DB data that were subsequently changed. The high stakes of MCC eligibility make it all the more important for DB to stabilize the methodology, make clear that posted data are subject to change, and make available both original and modified data sets.

In the World Bank Group, DB plays an indirect role in assessing countries' policy frameworks. Six of the 10 DB indicators are used as "guideposts" (along with Investment Climate Assessments and other sources) to assist country teams in determining country scores on "Business Regulatory Environment," one of the 16 criteria of the Country Policy and Institutional Assessment (CPIA), the most important (but not the only) determinant of allocations to International Development Association (IDA) countries.[12] In addition, the DB's *employing workers* indicator is one of several guideposts for the CPIA's social protection and labor criterion, even though this indicator captures only the administrative burden to firms of issues such as retraining and severance pay, rather than a broad assessment of a country's social protection policies. The extent to which the guideposts (including the DB indicators) influence the CPIA scores will be reviewed in a forthcoming IEG evaluation of the CPIA.[13]

The "IDA results framework"—a tool to help IDA donors track development results in IDA countries—reports DB numbers on the time and cost to start a business as 2 of the 14 "outcome" indicators (World Bank 2007b). This results framework is an ex-post reporting mechanism and is used neither to allocate resources nor to guide IDA programs ex-ante.

Continuous revisions to the DB data and unavailability of previously published data sets limit its usefulness for research.

The DB indicators are used to monitor progress of lending operations, including development policy loans that deal with private sector development issues. In 6 of 11 countries reviewed by this evaluation, such operations used DB indicators as one of the key monitoring indicators for specific components.[14] For instance, the time and cost of starting a business is used to monitor progress of one component of Tanzania's Private Sector Competitiveness Project.

DB plays a role in determining eligibility for grants made by the United States' Millennium Challenge Corporation.

An Addition to the Bank's Toolkit

DB has helped to define a new role for the Bank in development assistance. A majority of the stakeholders interviewed noted that DB is one of the first initiatives to develop objective (that is, non-perception-based) cross-country data, and thus fill a critical gap in knowledge.[15] It is a "knowledge" product, as distinct from analysis done to support lending and related conditionality. DB draws on the Bank's unique position to assemble information on a global scale. While other indicators, such as the World Development Indicators, cover many countries, DB incorporates indicators that are defined specifically enough to determine actionable steps.

DB does not affect the Bank's resource allocation decisions.

The DB model—use of a standard case methodology, expert informants, and rankings—is being replicated in other indicators. For instance, the Logistical Performance Index developed by the World Bank's Trade Group ranks the quality of infrastructure, customs procedures, and logistic costs in 150 countries based on information from freight forwarders, transporters, and officials. Other efforts to replicate

Among the Bank's knowledge tools, DB is one of the first to introduce indicators aimed at defining actionable steps.

this model in the financial sector are under way.

To what extent can the Bank scale up or replicate the DB model in other areas of development? Many development issues lack the DB indicators' critical characteristics of a widely accepted and linear trajectory for improvement and a clear definition of what constitutes a reform. The Bank should leverage the DB methodology in areas that share these characteristics.

Chapter 5

Wig shop owner using laptop. Photo reproduced by permission of Cat Gwynn/Corbis.

Findings and Recommendations

Doing Business has contributed to the development landscape in three main ways. For country authorities, it sheds a bright, sometimes unflattering, light on regulatory aspects of their business climate. For business interests, it has helped to catalyze debates and dialogue about reform. For the Bank Group, it demonstrates an ability to provide global knowledge, independent of resource transfer and conditionality. The annual exercise generates information that is relevant and useful. But it has several weaknesses in process, content, and presentation that should be rectified soon if it is to maintain its credibility and usefulness.

The Framework Underlying the DB Indicators

The DB indicators are anchored in research that links characteristics of the regulatory environment to firm performance, and thence to macroeconomic outcomes. Although some research has convincingly demonstrated these associations, any research relating the regulatory environment to economic outcomes is necessarily partial. It does not capture the influence of all the other determinants, nor can it pin down the direction of causality. Even where an association *is* demonstrated, the policy implications are not self-evident, since regulations deliver benefits as well as costs. What is good for a firm (or firms) may not be good for firms at large, or the economy and society as a whole. The right balance for any country is a matter of political choice.

The DB exercise reflects these inherent limitations. As an exercise in cross-country comparison, it is not intended to capture country nuances and nonlinear relationships. It measures selected dimensions of the regulatory environment, some of which are bound to be irrelevant in some countries. It notes the costs of regulation but not the benefits. Seven of DB's 10 indicators presume that lessening regulation is always desirable, whether a country starts with a little or a lot of regulation. These limitations do not invalidate the exercise, because the scope and thrust of DB are consistent with a credible view that less burdensome business regulation is associated with better private sector performance. But they underscore the need to use caution in interpreting the results and for the DB indicators to be used in conjunction with complementary tools such as Investment Climate Assessments.

DOING BUSINESS: AN INDEPENDENT EVALUATION

The Scope of the Indicators

The indicators are consistent with their claim of measuring the content of rules and laws, as distinct from perception. The dimensions of the regulatory environment that they measure are important in the aggregate—but not all indicators are important in all countries. The relevance of an indicator in a particular country setting will depend partly on the extent to which the law is actually applied, which DB does not measure. The impact of a given reform will likewise vary across countries. While the addition of new indicators would expand the coverage of issues addressed, by itself this would not make the DB indicators more reliable or useful. The more immediate challenge is to enhance reliability of the underlying information, as discussed below.

The *employing workers* indicator is consistent with the letter of ILO provisions, but four measures do not reflect their spirit. Beyond these minimum standards, the DB criteria give lower scores to countries that have opted for policies of greater job protection. There are a few systematic differences in country rankings associated with legal origins in civil or common law. These are consistent with the stated ideas behind the DB framework and they have little impact on the overall rankings or the validity of the exercise. DB's measurement of the total tax rate is anomalous because unlike DB's other subindicators, it does not measure regulatory burden alone. It derives from a country's fiscal requirements and policy context. Moreover, the complexity of this subindicator necessitates DB's reliance on PwC as virtually the sole informant—a reliance that entails risk to the exercise. Because tax rates are important for investors, information about them should be collected and presented, but not included in the rankings.

Inaccurate nomenclature and overstated claims of the indicators' explanatory power have provoked considerable criticism from stakeholders. DB reports should seek to retain their clarity while using less sweeping language.

Reliability of Information

DB has created a unique information-gathering process based on a global network of volunteer informants. This process is capable of generating reliable data, but three areas of vulnerability need to be addressed.

First, the database is too dependent on a small number of informants, with some data points generated by just one or two firms. For the information about taxes, DB's exclusive reliance on a single global firm for both the underlying methodology and the data from 142 countries poses extra risks. The number and diversity of informants should be increased and their information validated more systematically. An increase in the informant base will require a systematic vetting process. Simplifying the questionnaire may also help to encourage more informants to contribute.

Second, DB makes easily available a great deal of data and explanatory material—arguably more than most comparable exercises. Yet it remains insufficiently transparent about the number and types of informants for each indicator in a country, the adjustments staff make to the information supplied by informants, and the changes made to previously published data. It does not adequately point out the possibilities of errors and biases.

Third, DB makes much of its country rankings. The rankings entail three weaknesses. Because most DB indicators presume that less regulation is better, it is difficult to tell whether the top-ranked countries have good and efficient regulations or simply inadequate regulation. The small informant base makes it difficult to measure confidence in the accuracy of the individual indicator values, and thus in the aggregate rankings. Finally, changes in a country's ranking depend importantly on where it sits on the distribution; small changes can produce large ranking jumps, and vice versa. These factors contribute to anomalies in rankings.

These issues may not in and of themselves jeopardize DB's reliability, but the lack of transparency about them undermines DB's credibility and goodwill. In addition, the lack of stability in the data and the failure to make available prior versions of data that have been adjusted limit DB's usefulness for research. DB's documents and presentations should include full explanations and cautions on these points.

Motivating and Designing Reforms

The DB indicators have been influential in motivating policy makers to discuss and consider business regulation issues. Its active dissemination in easy-to-understand language permits widespread press coverage and generates interest from businesses, NGOs, and senior policy makers.

The DB indicators have had less influence on the choice and design of specific reform programs. Most Bank Group staff and country stakeholders report that they draw on a range of analytical material to determine the nature, sequence, and direction of reforms; the DB indicators have limited use in this regard. There is little evidence that the DB indicators have distorted policy priorities in the countries or in the Bank Group's programs, or that countries have implemented reforms with insincere motives. The DB indicators do not play a role in IDA's resource allocation process. Their use by the United States' MCC as a basis for resource allocation poses

some risk to the MCC because of the continuous revision of DB data after publication.

Implications for the Bank Group

In addition to the findings for the design and use of the DB exercise itself, the evaluation has generated two implications for the Bank Group more broadly.

The Bank Group, by so prominently recognizing DB's highly ranked countries, may be inadvertently signaling that it values reduced regulatory burdens more than its other development goals. Although the Bank Group's approach entails helping countries achieve a wide range of objectives, it has no comparable way of celebrating improvements in other important development outcomes such as poverty reduction, public sector effectiveness, or the Millennium Development Goals.

The DB exercise has demonstrated that a cross-country ranking exercise can be effective in spurring dialogue and motivating interest and action. Can it be extended to other topics and issues? It can be used for issues that meet two conditions. There must be measurable indicators to serve as agreed proxies for the target

---

Box 5.1: If DB Were to Be Extended to Other Topics

Bank Group management may consider building on DB's experience by creating indicators on additional development topics. If so, the evaluation offers five lessons:

- *Choose what to measure and start small:* Use existing or new research to identify a few issues within a sector/theme that can serve as at least partial proxies for development. Then specify some quantitative variables that can be measured relatively easily, have an intuitive appeal, and are easily understood. This implies accepting that the indicators will be limited in scope, not comprehensive.

- *Look for efficiency in data collection and processing:* Data collection methods need to be simple. Use an appropriately diverse range of expert informants and provide informants with a common reference point such as a hypothetical scenario.

- *Identify target audience:* Country benchmarking can be an effective door-opener and motivate a wider dialogue. Consider in advance who the indicators should aim to influence and who could participate in the dialogue.

- *Create and maintain competitive pressure:* Any indicator can be effective only to the extent it is widely communicated and understood by the target audience and can generate competition among countries and pressure to reform. The DB's assertive marketing and communication strategy combined with its use of rankings helped to generate and maintain country interest.

- *Do not overstate the implications of the rankings:* Cross-country rankings inherently miss country-specific issue nuances. They have to be used in conjunction with other analyses to help countries determine the direction, nature, and sequence of reforms.

outcomes. And the direction of improvement must be the same across countries starting at widely different levels. For many development issues, the trajectories for change are not linear, but U-shaped. (For example, automated teller machines are an indicator of efficient financial services. At an earlier stage of development, more automated teller machines are better, but in mature economies, too many can be a sign of inadequate interbank networking). Further lessons from the evaluation are distilled in box 5.1.

Recommendations

1. **To improve the credibility and quality of the rankings,** the DB team should:

   a. **Take a strategic approach** to selecting and increasing the number of informants:

      – Establish and disclose selection criteria for informants.

      – Focus on the indicators with fewest informants and countries with the least reliable information.

      – Formalize the contributions of the supplemental informants by having them fill out the questionnaire.

      – Involve Bank Group staff more actively to help identify informants.

   b. **Be more transparent** on the following aspects of the process:

      – *Informant base:* Disclose the number of informants for each indicator at the country level, differentiating between those who complete questionnaires and those who provide "supplemental" information.

      – *Changes in data:* Disclose a list of all data corrections and changes as they are made. Explain their effect on the rankings, and, to facilitate research, make available all previously published data sets.

      – *Use of the indicators:* Be clear about the limitations in the use of the indicators for a broader policy dialogue on a country's development priorities.

   c. **Revise the *paying taxes* indicator to include only measures of administrative burden.** Since the tax rate is an important part of the business climate, DB should continue to collect and present simple information on corporate tax rates, but exclude it from the rankings (as it does for the information it collects on nonwage labor costs in the *employing workers* indicator). A wider range of informants should also be engaged in supplying information for the *paying taxes* indicator.

2. **To make its reform analysis more meaningful,** the DB team should:

   a. **Make clear that DB measures improvements to regulatory burdens and costs,** which is only one dimension of any overall reform effort of the investment climate for private sector growth. The DB indicators measure reductions in regulatory burdens and should be recognized and rewarded as such. These improvements should not be characterized as reforms of the overall business climate, which reflects a number of non-DB-measured aspects, as noted in figure 1.1.

   b. **Trace the impact of DB reforms at the country level.** The DB team should work with country units to analyze the effects of implementing the reforms measured by the DB indicators (such as revised legislation or streamlined processes) on: (i) firm performance, (ii) perceptions of business managers on related regulatory burdens, and (iii) the efficiency of the regulatory environment in the country.

3. **To plan additions to or modifications of the indicators,** the DB team should:

   a. **Use Bank analyses to drive the choice of DB indicators.** These would include Business Enterprise Surveys, Investment Climate Assessments, and other relevant Bank analyses to assess what stakeholders deem to be important priorities for domestic private sector growth. The DB team should use such analyses to determine the choice of new indicators and periodically reassess its current set.

   b. **Pilot and stabilize the methodology before including new indicators in rankings.** Frequent changes in methodology make comparison across time less meaningful. New indicators should be piloted—that is, data collected and published for comment, but not factored into the rankings—until the methodology is validated and stabilized.

Appendixes

Village shop at dusk, lit by solar panels, Sri Lanka. Photo courtesy of Dominic Sansoni/World Bank.

This evaluation covers the period from the first DB report published in 2004 to the report published in September 2007. Data analysis is based on a download of the full data set from the DB Web site in August 2007 and, where noted, as subsequently revised in October 2007. Where appropriate, updating references are made to the 2008 report. In all, the evaluation interviewed 167 individuals: 72 Bank Group staff, 40 DB informants, 22 government officials, and 33 other stakeholders, including representatives from the private sector, international donor agencies, and academia.

The evaluation used the following methods to gather evidence:

1. Analysis of DB Ratings and Underlying Raw Data

(a) *Range, means, and distribution of subindicators and indicators and simulation of reforms:* The evaluation calculated the range, means, frequency distribution, and other characteristics of DB data. The pair-wise correlations among indicators and subindicators were calculated. A simulation was conducted of how rankings would vary for a given change in the underlying indicator (see appendix B for details).

(b) *Revisions in prior data:* The DB team periodically revises data for prior years. The evaluation assessed the revisions made to the data published in the DB 2007 report as part of the process of the DB 2008 report. It assessed the volume and reasons for the changes and their impact on the indicators and overall EODB ranking, as well as on the identification of reformer countries. This analysis in reflected in appendix C.

(c) *Patterns by legal system:* The evaluation analyzed patterns in the values of the subindicators for countries with particular legal systems according to legal origin. The results of this analysis are presented in appendix D.

2. Country Case Studies

Thirteen country case studies were used as the basis for detailed quantitative analysis and to obtain qualitative information from interviews with Bank and IFC staff, private sector representatives, government officials, and donors (see table A.1). Seven of the countries were randomly selected from the total 175 countries covered in *Doing Business 2007*. An additional 6 were randomly selected from the subset of 19 countries that DB identified as "top reformers" in the 2006 and 2007 reports.[1]

For all the case studies, evaluators interviewed key Bank and IFC staff and stakeholders in person, by telephone, and/or by e-mail, using uniform interview protocols developed by the evaluation team (see appendix E for a sample of the interview protocols). Telephone calls were used as appropri-

Table A.1: Case Study Countries

Country case studies	Top reformer case studies
Albania	China
Algeria	Netherlands
Burundi	Peru
Moldova	Rwanda
Mongolia	Tanzania
Nigeria	Vietnam
Spain	

ate to clarify and supplement information received by e-mail. In addition, the evaluation visited Moldova and conducted 12 face-to-face interviews with governmental and nongovernmental stakeholders. The mission observed the DB team's videoconference presentation of the 2008 report to an audience in Chisinau on November 2, 2007. The mission also visited the Netherlands and interviewed four country stakeholders. For the case studies, the evaluation conducted a total of 100 interviews: 55 Bank and IFC staff, 22 government officials, and 23 other stakeholders, including representatives from the private sector, international agencies, NGOs, and research think tanks. The evaluation team interviewed IFC staff working on investment climate issues in the Private Enterprise Partnership (PEP) facilities and FIAS, as well as Bank staff working on private sector development issues and relevant projects and analytical and advisory activities (AAA), as well as at least one person from the country management team. These staff directed IEG to the two to three people in the government and donor community most knowledgeable about the DB exercise.

The case studies also included reviews of Bank documents, including Country Assistance Strategies, Investment Climate Assessments, economic and sector work, and project documents related to private sector development, as well as other assessments of the business environment from the World Economic Forum, Heritage Founda-

tion, and the Economist Intelligence Unit. The team reviewed internal correspondence from operational staff commenting on the DB process and indicators for the 2007 and 2008 reports.

3. Validation Exercise

The evaluation reviewed the data collection process in the seven country case study countries through a review of the completed questionnaires and comparison with the final published data, and interviews with informants based on standard guidelines.

In the seven country case study countries, a total of 68 informants are listed by DB for the 5 focus indicators (see table A.2). The evaluation team made at least three attempts to contact each of them and succeeded in contacting and interviewing 59 percent (40 informants) by phone or by e-mail. Of the 28 informants who could not be contacted, 19 had unusable contact information or did not respond after repeated attempts, 7 had left their position, and 2 had died.

The evaluation also analyzed the composition and characteristics of the informants for all 175 countries in *Doing Business 2007* (see chapter 2 for details on the findings from the validation exercise).

4. In-Depth Analysis of Five Indicators

For assessing the relevance of the indicators to

Table A.2: Reach of the Validation Exercise

Country	Questionnaire informants	Supplemental informants	Total	Percent of all questionnaire informants	Percent of all informants (questionnaire and supplemental)	Percent of all informants (68 total)
Albania	5	2	7	62	88	10
Algeria	3	1	4	38	36	6
Burundi	2	2	4	33	36	6
Moldova	3	1	4	43	57	6
Mongolia	2	1	3	25	38	4
Nigeria	7	3	10	70	63	15
Spain	7	1	8	35	38	12
Total	**29**	**11**	**40**	**AVG 44**	**AVG 51**	**AVG 59**

countries and relevant intermediate outcomes, the evaluation focused its analysis on five broadly representative DB dimensions: *starting a business, employing workers, enforcing contracts, getting credit,* and *paying taxes.* The team reviewed relevant literature and interviewed 8 (non-country-specific) Bank Group staff and 10 other subject matter experts.

5. Portfolio Review

The evaluation reviewed the portfolio of Bank investment operations and IFC technical assistance and advisory services to identify patterns and trends in the Bank's support of private sector development, and specifically the areas related to the 10 dimensions of the business environment measured by DB between fiscal years 2004 and 2007.

Project descriptions do not explicitly identify the costs related to the dimensions covered by DB. To estimate the volume of Bank operations related to the 10 dimensions covered by DB, the evaluation team selected 11 (of a total of 71)

themes that correspond most directly with the investment climate issues covered by DB. As these themes cover all sectors, the review identified 130 projects that were mapped to the Financial and Private Sector Development Sector Board and approved between fiscal years 2004 and 2007.

As depicted in figure A.1, the Bank provided $9.8 billion in loans and grants for the 130 projects mapped to the Financial and Private Sector Development (FPD) Sector Board. Not all of this funding was related to strictly DB-measured indicators. Regulation and competition policy, small and medium-size enterprise support, and export development and competitiveness have the most funding and account for nearly three-quarters (72 percent) of the total $4.8 billion allocated to the 11 DB-related themes.

To estimate how much IFC allocated to technical assistance and advisory services for DB-related areas, the evaluation reviewed the six subareas of business lines that correspond most directly with

Figure A.1: Financial and Private Sector Development (FPD) Sector Board Projects by Theme, Fiscal 2004–07

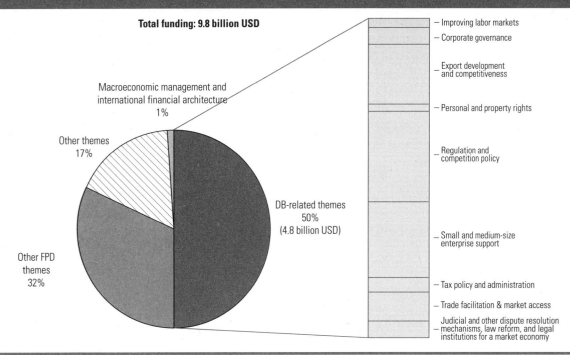

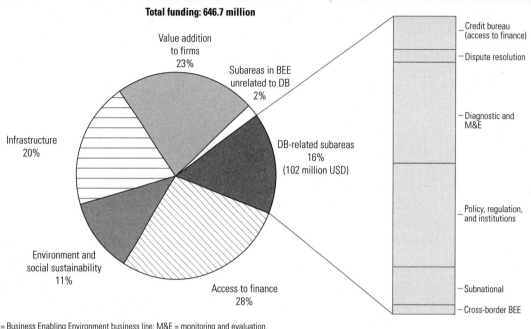

Figure A.2: IFC Technical Advisory Funding, Fiscal 2004–07

Total funding: 646.7 million

Value addition
to firms
23%

Subareas in BEE
unrelated to DB
2%

Infrastructure
20%

DB-related subareas
16%
(102 million USD)

Environment and
social sustainability
11%

Access to finance
28%

Credit bureau
(access to finance)

Dispute resolution

Diagnostic and
M&E

Policy, regulation,
and institutions

Subnational

Cross-border BEE

Note: BEE = Business Enabling Environment business line; M&E = monitoring and evaluation.

the DB indicators. These were one from the Access to Finance business line (credit bureau) and five from the Business Enabling Environment (BEE) business line (dispute resolution, diagnostic and monitoring and evaluation [M&E], policy, regulation and institutions, subnational, and cross-border). As shown in figure A.2, of the 906 technical assistance projects undertaken by IFC between 2004 and 2007, $102 million (16 percent of a total of $647 million) were spent on these six subareas. Diagnostic and M&E and policy, regulation, and institutions account for more than two-thirds of this amount.

6. Literature Review

The evaluation commissioned a review of literature on the theoretical and empirical underpin-

nings for the approach adopted by DB. The same review also undertook a cross-country econometric analysis to: (1) assess the consistency of the indicators with other Bank and externally generated indicators of investment climate and business regulation, and (2) determine correlations between the DB indicators and the economic variables that one may expect to be affected using both aggregate and firm-level data. This background paper is available upon request and will be made available on the IEG Web site.

7. Use and Communications

The evaluation interviewed staff at the Bank, IFC-FIAS, and the MCC and reviewed pertinent documents in connection with how the DB indicators are used in various operational contexts.

APPENDIX B: HOW EQUITABLY DO THE RANKINGS REWARD REFORMS?

Each of DB's 10 indicators uses cardinal values for its subindicators: time, cost, number of procedures, and so on to create a ranking. These cardinal values are ranked according to their respective percentiles in each of the subindicator distributions. The subindicator percentiles are then averaged to come up with an indicator-level percentile; the 10 indicator percentiles are then averaged to generate the overall ease of doing business (EODB) ranking.[1]

The use of several levels of ordinal rankings obscures the underlying cardinal values. That is, the magnitude of the difference between the countries ranked, say, fifty-ninth and sixtieth is not necessarily the same as that between those ranked first and second. Figure B.1 illustrates this point by showing the frequency distribution for the total tax rate as a share of profits, a subindicator of *paying taxes*. There is a 5.1 percentage point difference between the top performer, Maldives, and the runner-up, Vanuatu. There is a 4.7 percentage point difference between the last and next-to-last countries in the distribution, Gambia and Burundi. However, the countries ranked fifty-ninth and sixtieth, Israel and Mozambique, are separated by just 0.1 of a percentage point (39.1 percent and 39.2 percent respectively), while there are 13 other countries accompanying them in the range between 37 percent and 40.3 percent.

Figure B.1: Difference between Ranks Can Vary

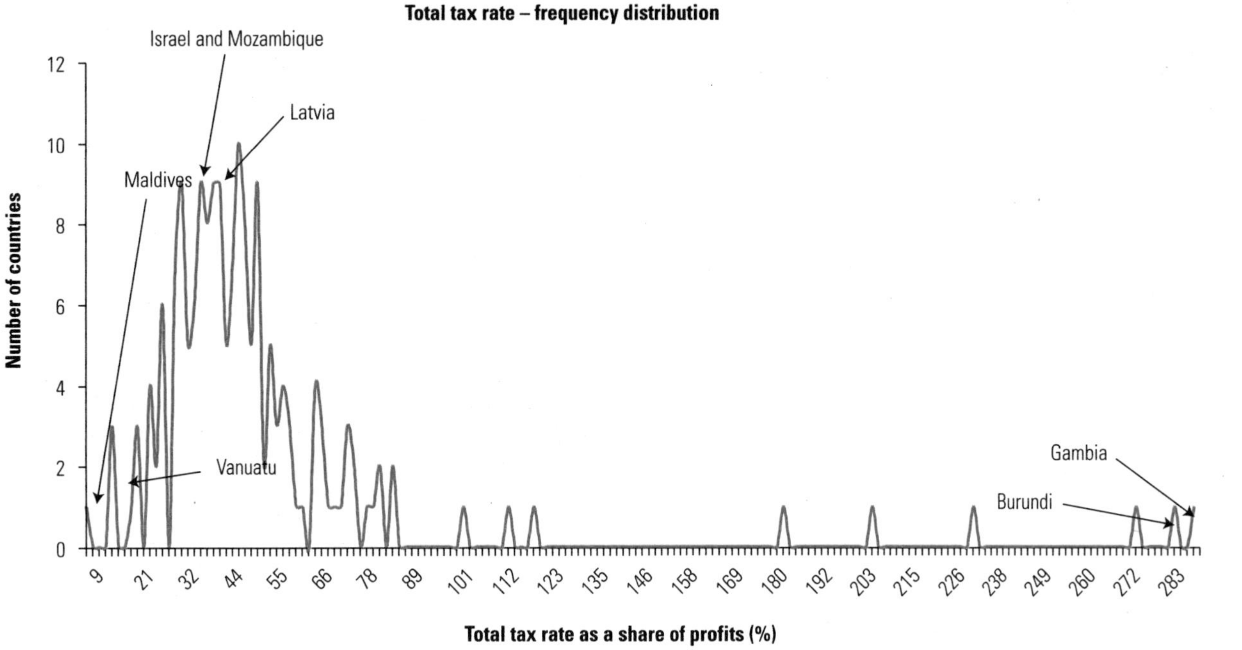

Total tax rate – frequency distribution

Table B.1: Countries in the Bottom Quartile on the *Paying Taxes* Indicator Need to Reduce Taxes More to Increase Rankings Relative to Countries in the 2nd and 3rd Quartiles

Country	Total tax rate 2007 (%)	Total tax rate 2008 (%)	Rank *paying taxes* 2007	Simulated rank with 2008 value	Difference in *paying taxes* rank
Latvia	43	33	52	35	17
Botswana	53	17	67	18	49
Kuwait	56	14	41	8	33
Belarus	186	144	175	175	0
Sierra Leone	277	234	138	137	1

A given change in a cardinal value, such as a reduction in the time needed for a procedure, is more likely to advance a country's rank (holding other countries' actions constant) if the country starts from a more concentrated segment of the distribution than if it starts from a more dispersed section. This arithmetic means that countries at the more dispersed parts of the distribution have to work harder to see changes in their overall rankings. Put differently, countries can make significant changes that do not improve their rankings if they are at the dispersed sections of the distribution for that indicator. The following three examples illustrate this asymmetry by simulating the change in rankings for a subindicator, holding the actions of the other countries constant.

Example 1: How much does the tax rate have to fall to improve ranking on *paying taxes*? As seen in figure B.1, the frequency distribution for total tax rate as a share of profits for all countries ranges from 9.3 percent in Maldives to 291.4 percent in Gambia.

Almost all the countries (165, or 94 percent) fall within one standard deviation from the mean. Table B.1 presents the results of simulations[2] after improvements in the total tax rate. Sierra Leone is in the dispersed segment at the bottom of the total tax rate distribution, right before Burundi and Gambia. Despite a 43 percentage point reduction in total tax rate, the country improved only one position in the simulated ranking for *paying taxes.* Belarus's substantial tax reduction likewise did not affect the simulated ranking. Latvia, by contrast, despite only reducing the total tax rate by 10 percentage points, improved 17 positions because it is situated in the most populated segment of the distribution. Kuwait and Botswana received an even stronger boost from their tax reduction because of the same effect.

Example 2: How does reducing the minimum capital requirement affect ranking on *starting a business*? In 2008, Egypt drastically reduced its minimum capital requirement—from 695 percent of

Table B.2: Despite Egypt's Efforts In Reducing the Minimum Capital Requirement, St. Kitts and Nevis, Gambia, and Macedonia Will Gain More on DB Rankings for Lower Reductions

Country	Minimum capital requirement 2007 (%)	Minimum capital requirement 2008 (%)	Rank, *starting a business,* 2007	Simulated rank, *starting a business,* with 2008 value	Difference in *starting a business* rank
Finland	27	8	19	13	6
St. Kitts and Nevis	45	0	105	61	44
Gambia	120	0	124	70	54
Macedonia, FYR	112	0	76	27	49
Egypt	695	13	125	92	33

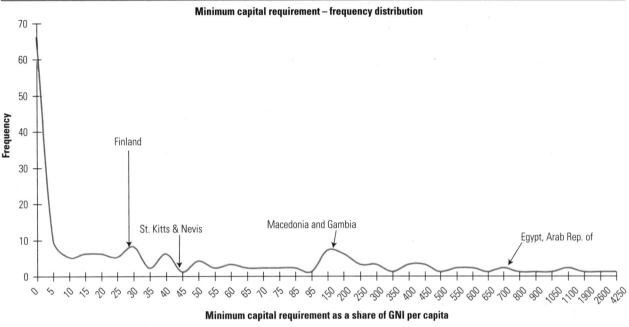

Figure B.2: Distribution of the Minimum Capital Requirement Subindicator for _Starting a Business_

Minimum capital requirement – frequency distribution

income per capita to just 13 percent. Holding other countries' actions constant, it would have generated a 33-position boost in the *starting a business* ranking (see table B.2). The distribution of this subindicator, as shown in figure B.2, is concentrated around zero. More than a third of the countries (66 of them) do not have a minimum capital requirement. Although Gambia, Macedonia, and Saint Kitts and Nevis all reduced the minimum capital requirement much less than Egypt in absolute terms in 2008, they would have

boosted their rankings more than Egypt would have. By eliminating the minimum capital requirement, these three countries tied with the other 66 countries for first place in this subindicator. In turn, this substantially reduced their total average percentile for *starting a business,* improving their ranking for this indicator. Finally, a country such as Finland was also able to advance in the rankings, although less than the other countries, because of the relative lack of concentration around it in the distribution.

Table B.3: Countries in the Bottom Quartile on the Minimum Capital Requirement Subindicator Need to Do Much More to Increase Rankings Relative to Countries in the 2nd and 3rd Quartiles

Country	Time (days) 2007	Time (days) 2008	Rank, *starting a business,* 2007	Simulated rank, *starting a business,* with 2008 value	Difference in *starting a business* rank
Estonia	35	7	51	27	24
Honduras	44	21	138	121	17
Mauritius	46	7	30	10	20
Mauritania	82	65	164	164	0
Lao PDR	163	103	73	73	0

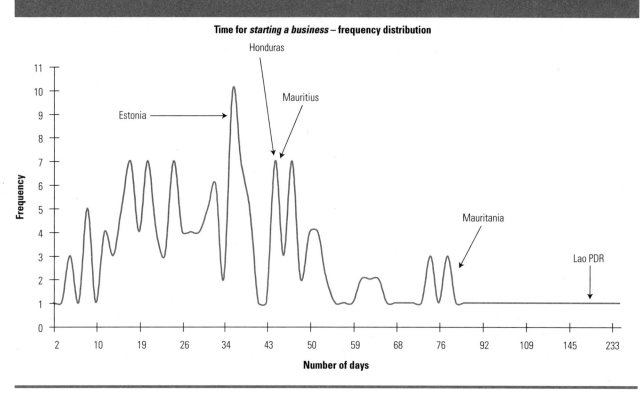

Figure B.3: Distribution of the Time to Start a Business

Time for *starting a business* – frequency distribution

Example 3: How does reducing the time to open a business improve *starting a business*? The Republic of Lao reduced the time to start a business by 60 days in 2008, yet such a change did not affect the simulated ranking for *starting a business* (table B.3). Mauritania experienced a similar result. Mauritius, by contrast, reduced the time by 41 days, thereby advancing 20 positions on *starting a business.* Honduras and Estonia, both in the middle segment of the distribution and close to the majority of countries, also made significant progress in the ranking for *starting a business.* Lao and Mauritania are at the bottom end of the distribution and fairly isolated (see figure B.3). A change in the sparsely populated bottom end will be less likely to improve the percentile ranking of a country in that subindicator. In turn, it will have little effect on the average of the percentiles of the subindicators, which gives the indicator ranking.

How Do Reforms Affect the EODB Distribution?

As mentioned above, the overall ranking of EODB is calculated from the average of the percentile scores for the 10 indicators. This final percentile average, the EODB percentile, is a distribution of cardinal values ranging from 0.08 for Singapore to 0.82 for the Democratic Republic of Congo (DRC). These values are then ranked in order, with the first position belonging to Singapore and the last to DRC. Figure B.4 shows the distribution of the EODB percentiles for 2007.

The simulations presented in tables B.1–B.3, aside from causing changes in the indicator ranking, also produced changes in the EODB ranking. Table B.4 summarizes some of these changes for selected countries. Mauritania and Sierra Leone are at the most dispersed part of the distribution and did not improve in the overall ranking, despite the improvements in time to start a business and total tax rate, respectively. Finland and Estonia also show no improvement. Botswana, in contrast, improved 6 positions thanks to its tax reform, and

Figure B.4: Average Percentile of 10 DB Indicators

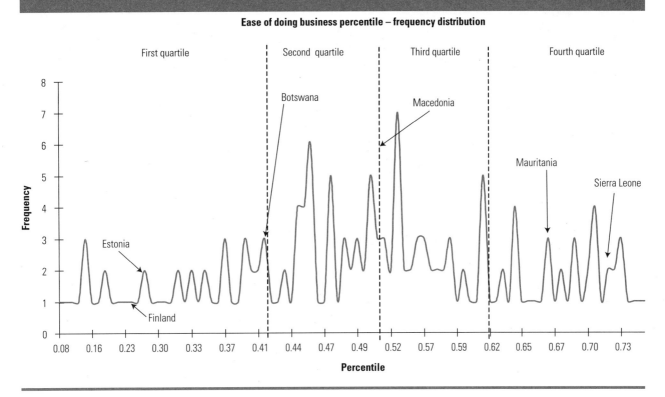

Ease of doing business percentile – frequency distribution

Macedonia improved 9 positions because of the elimination of the minimal capital requirement, because both countries are located in the more tightly distributed portions of the indicator.

Thus, a considerable improvement in the absolute value of a subindicator might not be enough to cause an improvement at the indicator level if that country is starting from a very low base. Countries in the most dispersed part of the distributions will need sizeable relative improvements in their subindicator values to catch up with the rest. This is the case for most of the countries in Africa.

Does the Ranking System Distort Reform Priorities?

It has been suggested that DB's use of rankings might create an incentive for countries to reform the areas where they are most likely to move up in the EODB ranking for the least reform effort. If this were the case, one would expect the highly concentrated subindicators to be associated with more reforms in a given year.[3] Table B.5 ranks DB's subindicators from most to least concentrated and shows the number of reforms associated with each of them in 2007.[4]

Table B.4: Despite Positive Changes, Countries at the Bottom and Top Quartiles Did Not Improve in Overall Rankings

Country	EODB 2007	Simulated EODB rank with 2008 reform	Difference in EODB rank
Finland	13	13	0
Estonia	17	16	1
Botswana	48	42	6
Macedonia, FYR	92	83	9
Mauritania	148	148	0
Sierra Leone	168	168	0

Table B.5: No Apparent Relationship between Tightness of Distribution and Reforms

Doing Business indicator	Subindicator	Number of countries in 1 standard deviation range	Percentage of countries in range	Frequency of reform in 2007
Paying taxes	Total tax rate	165	94	23
Starting a business	Minimum capital requirement	164	94	7
	Time	164	94	7
Employing workers	Firing costs	162	93	5
Dealing with licenses	Cost	158	90	9
Starting a business	Cost	158	90	5
Protecting investors	Time	158	90	2
Registering property	Time	150	86	6
Dealing with licenses	Procedures	149	85	12
Employing workers	Rigidity of hours	146	83	4
Starting a business	Procedures	138	79	28
Dealing with licenses	Time	135	77	3
Trading across borders	Time to export	134	77	17
Getting credit	Legal rights index	131	75	24
Enforcing contracts	Time	131	75	7
Trading across borders	Documents for export	129	74	10
Paying taxes	Payments	128	73	12
Registering property	Cost	127	73	14
	Procedures	126	72	7
Protecting investors	Disclosure index	124	71	9
Getting credit	Credit information index	123	70	13
Closing a business	Recovery rate	117	67	12
Protecting investors	Director liability index	117	67	4
	Shareholders suits index	116	66	3
Enforcing contracts	Procedures	115	66	20
Employing workers	Difficulty of firing index	113	65	1
	Difficulty of hiring index	109	62	2
Average		137	78	10
Median		131	75	7
Correlation between % of countries in range and number of reforms				0.01

The total tax rate is the third-most-frequent area of reform, and it has the tightest distribution of all the subindicators, with 94 percent of the countries' rankings within one standard deviation from the mean. But the two most popular areas for reform—number of procedures to start a business and legal rights of creditors and debtors—are not among the most tightly distributed. The correlation between tightness of distribution and frequency of reforms is almost nonexistent (0.01), offering no support to the hypothesis that the ranking arithmetic is distorting reforms. Alternative hypotheses are that governments implement reforms that are politically or administratively easier, or the ones they think most relevant.

APPENDIX C: DIFFERENCES BETWEEN DATA IN 2007 DB REPORT AND DB WEB SITE (OCTOBER 2007) FOR SAME DATA COLLECTION PERIOD

	Number of differences	Reason	Written explanation	Differences of 10% or less
Starting a business				
Procedures (number)	24	Data corrections	⎤	10
Time (days)	32	Data corrections	⎱ Not found	13
Cost (% of income per capita)	19	Data corrections	⎱	5
Minimum capital (% of income per capita)	11	Data corrections	⎦	0
Dealing with licenses[a]				
Procedures (number)	130	Methodology change/ data corrections	⎤	—
Time (days)	148	Methodology change/ data corrections	⎱ Page 68 of *Doing Business 2008*	—
Cost (% of income per capita)	106	Methodology change/ data corrections	⎦	—
Employing workers				
Difficulty of hiring index (0–100)	44	Methodology change	⎤	—
Rigidity of hours index (0–100)	40	Methodology change	⎱ Page 68 of *Doing Business 2008*	—
Difficulty of firing index (0–100)	46	Methodology change	⎱	—
Firing cost (weeks of salary)	28	Methodology change	⎦	—
Registering property				
Procedures (number)	10	Data corrections	⎤	1
Time (days)	17	Data corrections	⎱ Not found	4
Cost (% of property value)	29	Data corrections	⎦	9
Getting credit				
Depth of credit information index (0–10)	12	Data corrections	⎱ Not found	—
Strength of legal rights index (0–10)	46	Data corrections	⎦	—
Protecting investors				
Extent of disclosure index (0–10)	34	Data corrections	⎤	—
Extent of director liability index (0–10)	23	Data corrections	⎱ Not found	—
Ease of shareholder suits index (0–10)	33	Data corrections	⎦	—

(*continues on the following page*)

	Number of differences	Reason	Written explanation	Differences of 10% or less
Paying taxes[a]				
Payments (number per year)	127	Methodology change/ data corrections	Page 78 of *Doing Business 2008*	—
Time (hours per year)	54	Methodology change/ data corrections		—
Total tax rate (% of profit)	160	Methodology change/ data corrections		—
Trading across borders				
Documents to export (number)	104	Data corrections	Not found	9
Time to export (days)	109	Data corrections		38
Cost to export (US$ per container)	121	Data corrections		40
Documents to import (number)	124	Data corrections		19
Time to import (days)	114	Data corrections		37
Cost to import (US$ per container)	116	Data corrections		34
Enforcing contracts[a]				
Procedures (number)	166	Methodology change/ data corrections	Page 68 of *Doing Business 2008*	—
Time (days)	78	Methodology change/ data corrections		—
Cost (% of claim)	157	Methodology change/ data corrections		—
Closing a business				
Recovery rate (cents on the dollar)	22	Data corrections	Not found	3

a. According to the DB team, for these three indicators, the methodology changes affect so many countries that it is difficult to separate corrected errors from metholodogy revisions.

There is a great body of literature hypothesizing that differences in economic prosperity can be traced to the legal systems of countries. Some research has posited that countries with a legal system originating in the English common law tradition have enjoyed greater per capita growth than countries whose legal systems originated in the French civil law tradition, deriving from the European civil codes, especially the Napoleonic Code. This appendix explores whether legal origins affect the performance of countries on the DB indicators. The results show that common law countries perform better in four indicators, yet differences wane in two of them as additional control variables are included.[1]

Regression analysis was performed using the 32 subindicators that feed the 10 indicators. The subindicators served as the dependent variable. The controls variables included were income per capita and a dummy variable for civil law legal origin. The results are displayed in table D.2. The 175 countries in *Doing Business 2007* were coded into five categories according to legal origin[2]: common law (59), civil law (76), German (20), Nordic (5), and Socialist (11). Four of the 175 countries were excluded because their legal origin was not clear. When testing for differences between common and civil law origin, the sample was limited to those 135 countries.

There are 4 indicators and 13 subindicators where civil law countries perform significantly worse than common law countries. These are:

- The four subindicators that comprise the *starting a business* indicator
- The director liability index and shareholder suits index that comprise *protecting investors*

- Three of the indicators for *employing workers:* rigidity of hiring index, rigidity of hours index, and rigidity of firing index
- The legal rights subindicator under the *getting credit* indicator.

In addition, the number of procedures and time under the *paying taxes* and the time under *dealing with licenses* indicators are significantly different, favoring common law countries. The only indicator that favors countries with a civil law origin is the credit information index in *getting credit*. This, according to Djankov and others (2006), can be attributed to the presence of a public credit registry in countries with a French civil law tradition. Differences in all other subindicators are not statistically significant.

What Explains the Differences?

The four subindicators in *starting a business*—number of procedures, time, cost, and minimum capital requirement—are significantly higher in French-origin countries. It is plausible that in the case of the first three, the differences are a result of the participation of notary publics in the business registration process.

The differences in *protecting investors* and *getting credit* could also be attributed to legal origin, since the Napoleonic Code deals with commercial procedures, among other issues. However, there are no statistically significant differences between the two groups of countries in any of the subindicators for *enforcing contracts,* which could have been plausibly attributed directly to differences in legal origin as well.

The differences in *employing workers* are not as

easy to understand, since the Napoleonic Code does not delve deeply into this issue. A general hypothesis could be that, on average, countries with a civil law tradition favor direct supervision of markets. In this case, civil law countries would prefer more government regulation to protect the rights of workers.

The differences in *paying taxes* are also not easy to understand, since the number of payments and the time it takes to file taxes would depend more on the efficiency of tax collection than legal origin. For instance, DB rewards countries with full online filing by counting the tax as paid once a year, even if the payment is more frequent.

Controlling for Additional Factors

As a second stage of the analysis, additional control variables were introduced to test the robustness of the differences in DB indicator rankings, specifically for the *employing workers* and *paying taxes* indicators. For example, the difference in ratings for the *employing workers* indicator may reflect the preference for greater social welfare, specifically in continental European countries. Similarly, on *paying taxes,* the differences may reflect the level of efficiency of the state. In sum, the differences based on legal origin for *employing workers* are somewhat less robust, and disappear for *paying taxes* once other factors are accounted for. (The analysis is summarized in table D.1 and detailed in Attachment D.1.)

Table D.1: Differences between Countries Based on Legal Origin on *Employing Workers* and *Paying Taxes* Wane after Adding Other Control Variables

Controls	Employing workers		
	Difficulty of hiring	Difficulty of firing	Rigidity of hours
1) None	Significant (99%)	Significant (99%)	Significant (99%)
2) Welfare variables (individually and together)	Not significant	Significant (99%)	Significant (99%)
3) Welfare variables (excluding small countries)	Significant (99%)	Not significant	Significant (99%)
4) Continental Europe	Significant (95%)	Significant (95%)	Significant (95%)
5) Income group (with welfare controls)			
• High income	Significant (95%)	Significant (95%)	Significant (95%)
• Upper-middle income	Not significant	Not significant	Significant (95%)
• Lower-middle income	Significant (95%)	Not significant	Significant (95%)
Controls	Paying taxes		
	No. of procedures	Time	Total tax rate
1) None	Significant (95%)	Significant (95%)	Not significant
2) Revenue collection proxy	Not significant	Not significant	Not significant

ATTACHMENT D.1: RESULTS OF REGRESSION ANALYSIS FOR TEST DIFFERENCES BASED ON LEGAL ORIGIN ON *EMPLOYING WORKERS* AND *PAYING TAXES*

Employing Workers

Controlling for welfare preferences. A possible explanation for the differences in *employing workers* could be the preferences for more social welfare in countries with a civil law tradition. To proxy for this, aside from income per capita, three additional control variables were introduced into the regression: (a) revenue as a share of GDP,[3] (b) tax revenue as a share of GDP, and (c) public health and education expenditures as a share of GDP.[4] When these are included individ-

ually in the regression, the difference between common and civil law legal origin countries is statistically significant (99 percent level) on two subindicators—difficulty of hiring and rigidity of hours. The significance of the differences in the difficulty of firing index depends on the control variable. The results do not change if revenue or tax revenue is used simultaneously with health and education spending in the regression.

Subindicator	Common vs. civil law legal origin subindicators for *employing workers*				Significance of difference between countries of common and civil law legal origin, controlling for income per capita and–		
	Scale (0 is best)	Common law average	Civil law average	Difference	Total revenue as share of GDP	Tax revenue as share of GDP	Public health and education spending as share of GDP
Difficulty of hiring index	0 – 100	17.0	46.2	29.2	0.99	0.99	0.99
Rigidity of hours index	0 – 100	20.7	48.7	28.0	0.99	0.99	0.99
Difficulty of firing index	0 – 100	20.4	40.0	19.6	Not significant	Not significant	0.99
Firing costs (weeks of wages)	0 – infinity	58.3	51.3	−7.0	Not significant	Not significant	Not significant
Number of observations		59	76		135	135	135

Creating a continental Europe origin group. The analysis has so far excluded Nordic (Denmark, Finland, Iceland, Norway, and Sweden) and German legal origin countries (Austria, Germany, Switzerland, and Eastern European countries). It can be argued that these countries might have similar preferences for the level of taxation and the provision of public goods as do French origin countries. Therefore, a new group was created, continental Europe, which

adds civil law legal origin countries with the German and Nordic countries of Europe. When this group is paired against common law countries, all differences in the values of the subindicators remained statistically significant, at least at a 95 percent level. That is, on average, countries with common law legal origin continue to perform better in all three subindicators—difficulty of hiring, of firing, and rigidity of hours.

| Subindicator | Scale (0 is best) | Continental European vs. English legal origin | | | Significance of difference between common law and continental European legal origin countries, controlling for income per capita and– | | |
		Common law average	Continental European legal origin average	Difference	Total revenue as share of GDP	Tax revenue as share of GDP	Public health and education spending as share of GDP
Difficulty of hiring index	0 – 100	17.0	43.3	26.3	0.99	0.99	0.99
Rigidity of hours index	0 – 100	20.7	49.2	28.5	0.99	0.99	0.99
Difficulty of firing index	0 – 100	20.4	38.3	17.9	0.95	0.95	0.99
Firing costs (weeks of wages)	0 – infinity	58.3	45.7	−12.6	Not significant	Not significant	Not significant
Number of observations		59	98		81	79	93

Stratifying by income group. The analysis was also performed by income group because associations with the welfare variables could be influenced by a country's revenue-collecting capacity. When controlling for the three welfare state proxies for the high-income-country group, differences between legal origins for the three subindicators are still statistically significant. The hypothesis that there are differences between the rigidity of labor laws in common law and continental European tradition high-income countries, as measured by DB, cannot be disproved.

| Subindicator | Scale (0 is best) | Limiting to high-income countries, N=30 | | | Significance of difference between common law and continental European legal origin countries, controlling for income per capita and– | | |
		Common law average	Continental European legal origin average	Difference	Total revenue as share of GDP	Tax revenue as share of GDP	Public health and education spending as share of GDP
Difficulty of hiring index	0 – 100	5.5	33.3	27.8	0.95	0.95	0.95
Rigidity of hours index	0 – 100	13.3	48.9	35.6	0.99	0.99	0.99
Difficulty of firing index	0 – 100	5.9	32.2	26.3	0.99	0.99	0.99
Firing costs (weeks of wages)	0 – infinity	37.6	29	−8.6	Not significant	Not significant	Not significant
Number of observations		12	18		23	24	24

When the analysis is performed on the upper-middle-income group, only the rigidity of hours index continues to be statistically higher in countries with a continental European origin.

| Subindicator | Scale (0 is best) | Limiting to upper-middle-income countries, N=34 | | | Significance of difference between common law and continental European legal origin countries, controlling for income per capita and– | | |
		Common law average	Continental European legal origin average	Difference	Total revenue as share of GDP	Tax revenue as share of GDP	Public health and education spending as share of GDP
Difficulty of hiring index	0 – 100	0 – 100	15.7	40.1	24.4	Not significant	Not significant
Rigidity of hours index	0 – 100	0 – 100	16.7	51.8	35.1	99	95
Difficulty of firing index	0 – 100	0 – 100	19.2	39.1	19.9	Not significant	Not significant
Firing costs (weeks of wages)	0 – infinity	0 – infinity	43.7	42.4	−1.3	Not significant	Not significant
Number of observations		12	22			20	18

However, in the case of lower-middle-income countries, it is the difficulty of hiring index that continues to be statistically greater in continental law origin countries after controlling for proxies of the welfare state. The significance of differences for the rigidity of hours index and the difficulty of firing index wane when welfare proxies are added.

| Subindicator | Scale (0 is best) | Limiting to lower-middle-income countries, N=47 | | | Significance of difference between common law and continental European legal origin countries, controlling for income per capita and– | | |
		Common law average	Continental European legal origin average	Difference	Total revenue as share of GDP	Tax revenue as share of GDP	Public health and education spending as share of GDP
Difficulty of hiring index	0 – 100	12.6	44.9	32.3	0.99	0.99	0.95
Rigidity of hours index	0 – 100	20	43	23	Not significant	Not significant	0.95
Difficulty of firing index	0 – 100	12.9	39.1	26.2	Not significant	Not significant	Not significant
Firing costs (weeks of wages)	0 – infinity	40.9	58.6	17.7	Not significant	Not significant	Not significant
Number of observations		14	33		25	24	24

In the low-income group, only the rigidity of hours index continues to be statistically higher in countries with a continental European origin after controlling for proxies of the welfare state. Nevertheless, in this particular group, the information for the control variables is scarce, which led to only using 13 or 17 observations in the regressions.

| Subindicator | Scale (0 is best) | Limiting to low-income countries, N=46 | | | Significance of difference between common law and continental European legal origin countries, controlling for income per capita and– | | |
		Common law average	Continental European legal origin average	Difference	Total revenue as share of GDP	Tax revenue as share of GDP	Public health and education spending as share of GDP
Difficulty of hiring index	0 – 100	27.2	51.4	24.2	Not significant	Not significant	Not significant
Rigidity of hours index	0 – 100	27.6	55.2	27.6	0.95	0.99	0.99
Difficulty of firing index	0 – 100	34.3	40.8	6.5	Not significant	Not significant	Not significant
Firing costs (weeks of wages)	0 – infinity	90.1	44.2	−45.9	Not significant	Not significant	Not significant
Number of observations		21	25		13	13	17

The results of these regressions do not change substantially when comparing common law versus civil law origin instead of continental European. Although some of the differences remain despite the inclusion of the control variables, the disappearance of some could be evidence that other factors aside from legal origin are important for explaining performance on the *employing workers* indicator.

Controlling for small-country outliers. Some small countries in the sample have unusually high values for the welfare control variables. Therefore, countries with a population of less than 2 million (the Bank's suggested definition of a small country) were excluded from the analysis. Once the proxies for the welfare state were added and small countries were excluded, the differences in the difficulty of firing index were not statistically significant.

Subindicator	Scale (0 is best)	Excluding countries with population of less than 2 million			Significance of difference between common law and continental European legal origin countries, controlling for income per capita and–		
		Common law average	Continental European legal origin average	Difference	Total revenue as share of GDP	Tax revenue as share of GDP	Public health and education spending as share of GDP
Difficulty of hiring index	0 – 100	18.9	44.2	25.3	0.99	0.99	0.99
Rigidity of hours index	0 – 100	23.3	49.4	26.1	0.99	0.99	0.99
Difficulty of firing index	0 – 100	25.3	36.1	10.8	Not significant	Not significant	Not significant
Firing costs (weeks of wages)	0 – infinity	76	43.8	−32.2	Not significant	Not significant	0.95
Number of observations		36	84		71	68	74

Paying Taxes: Controlling for Additional Factors

Two of the subindicators for *paying taxes,* number of payments and time, are statistically significantly higher in civil law countries than in common law countries. However, these differences could be attributed to the government's efficiency in tax collection. When an additional control variable, tax revenue as a share of GDP, is introduced into the regression, the differences cease to exist.

Subindicator	Scale	Common law average	Civil law average	Difference	Controlling for income per capita and tax revenue as share of GDP
Payments (number)	0 – infinity	28.9	37.2	8.3	Not significant
Time (hours)	0 – infinity	207.1	314.5	107.4	Not significant
Total tax rate (% profit)	0 – infinity	46.9	57.3	10.4	Not significant

Table D.2: Regression Results for Common and Civil Law Countries at the Subindicator Level

Indicator	Subindicator	Scale	Common law average	Civil law average	Difference	Significance of difference after controlling for income per capita - Oct. 2007
Starting a business	Procedures (number)	0 – infinity	8.2	10.9	2.6	0.99
	Time (days)	0 – infinity	37.8	64.2	26.4	0.95
	Cost (% of income per capita)	0 – infinity	44.4	96.3	51.9	0.99
	Min. capital (% of income per capita)	0 – infinity	16.0	154.1	138.1	0.99
Dealing with licenses	Procedures (number)	0 – infinity	16.5	18.6	2.1	Not significant
	Time (days)	0 – infinity	190.8	231.4	40.6	0.95
	Cost (% of income per capita)	0 – infinity	539.6	693.7	154.1	Not significant
Employing workers	Difficulty of hiring index	0 (best) –100 (worst)	17.0	46.2	29.2	0.99
	Rigidity of hours index	0 (best) –100 (worst)	20.7	48.7	28.0	0.99
	Difficulty of firing index	0 (best) –100 (worst)	20.4	40.0	19.6	0.99
	Firing costs (weeks of wages)	0 – infinity	58.3	51.3	−7.0	Not significant
Registering property	Procedures (number)	0 – infinity	6.2	6.5	0.3	Not significant
	Time (days)	0 – infinity	78.3	88.7	10.4	Not significant
	Cost (% of property value)	0 – infinity	6.9	8.4	1.5	Not significant
Getting credit	Credit information index	0 (worst) – 6 (best)	1.9	2.8	0.9	0.99
	Legal rights index	0 (worst) – 10 (best)	5.3	3.4	−1.9	0.99
Protecting investors	Disclosure index	0 (worst) – 10 (best)	4.9	4.8	−0.1	Not significant
	Director liability index	0 (worst) – 10 (best)	5.5	3.3	−2.1	0.99
	Shareholder suits index	0 (worst) – 10 (best)	6.5	4.7	−1.8	0.99
Paying taxes	Payments (number)	0 – infinity	28.9	37.2	8.3	0.95
	Time (hours)	0 – infinity	207.1	314.5	107.4	0.99
	Total tax rate (% profit)	0 – infinity	46.9	57.3	10.4	Not significant
Trading across borders	Documents for export (number)	0 – infinity	7.1	7.7	0.6	Not significant
	Time for export (days)	0 – infinity	25	29.6	4.6	Not significant
	Cost to export (US$ per container)	0 – infinity	1,128.1	1,298.6	170.5	Not significant
	Documents for import (number)	0 – infinity	8.3	9	0.7	Not significant
	Time for import (days)	0 – infinity	30.2	35.7	5.5	Not significant
	Cost to import (US$ per container)	0 – infinity	1,340.4	1,529.7	189.3	Not significant
Enforcing contracts	Procedures (number)	0 – infinity	38.1	39.1	1.0	Not significant
	Time (days)	0 – infinity	609.2	672.7	63.5	Not significant
	Cost (% of debt)	0 – infinity	33.2	40.9	7.7	Not significant
Closing a business	Recovery rate (cents on the dollar)	0 to $1.00	32.2	24.1	−8.0	Not significant

Note: N = civil law, 76: common law, 59; significant levels set at 95 percent or higher.

Appendix E.1: Interview Protocol for Doing Business Informants

[Greeting] I am calling on behalf of the World Bank's Independent Evaluation Group (IEG), which reports directly to the Board of Directors of the World Bank. The IEG is undertaking an evaluation of the World Bank Group's DB indicators.

I'm calling/contacting you because you are listed as an informant to the DB survey in Country X. As part of the evaluation, we are reviewing the process for collecting the data used in the DB report. We would very much value your views about the process and information collected. Your contribution is important for enhancing the future work of the World Bank Group.

This interview will about 20 minutes. Please be assured that your views will remain anonymous, and responses to this survey will not be attributed to you personally, or to your organization.

Background Information

a) What are the topics/questions that DB asks you to provide information on? What is your professional experience with these topic(s)?

b) How you were approached to participate? When did you first participate and how many times have you taken part?

c) Why do you participate?

d) How long did it take you to answer the survey, including time spent by colleagues or subordinates?

Validity of Assumptions

e) The DB survey presents a business case or a standard firm as the basis for your responses. In your opinion, are the assumptions described in the survey representative of a typical firm in your country? Why or why not?

f) In your judgment, how many firms fitting this assumption have used your services?

g) If you had to change the assumptions to make them more consistent with your country's realities, which assumptions would you change and why? And how would these changes affect your answers?

Survey Content and Structure

h) In your view, do the questions asked in the survey capture the essence of the business climate challenges on the topic? Are the questions focusing on the right aspects?

i) Do you have any other comments about the structure of the survey?

Validity of Information in DB Report

j) Have you seen the data published in the last DB report for your topic(s) or your country? Do you agree with the information?

k) In your view, do you think the DB report captures the changes in laws and regulations from one year to the next appropriately? Why or Why not?

Closing:

l) How useful has the Doing Business exercise been in your country? Please explain.

m) Is there anything else you would like to add about the DB survey process or report?

Appendix E.2: Interview Protocol for Policy Makers and Senior Government Officials

Introduction

We are writing on behalf of the World Bank's Independent Evaluation Group (IEG), which reports directly to the Board of Directors of the World Bank. The IEG is undertaking an evaluation of the World Bank's DB indicators. An important aspect of our work is to determine the relevance and the use of the DB indicators to the government and policy makers in developing countries. Your contribution is important for enhancing the future work of the World Bank Group.

Our survey will take about 45 minutes to complete. Please be assured that your views will remain anonymous, and responses will not be attributed to you personally.

I. Background:

a) In order of importance, please tell us, what, in your view, are the three factors affecting or impeding the growth of domestic private sector enterprises?

b) What issues have you or your government raised with donors, including the World Bank Group, regarding the development of the domestic private sector?

II. Relevance of the DBI:

c) Are you aware of the Doing Business indicators published by the World Bank Group? (Yes/No)

d) The Doing Business indicators, the subject of this evaluation, present information on 10 aspects of the business climate. For each, please tell us how important each of these are to enhancing the environment for domestic enterprises. Please use a scale of 1–4 where 1 = Very Important, 2 = Important, 3 = Slightly Important, and 4 = Not important.

Aspects	1. Very important	2. Important	3. Slightly important	4. Not important	Comments
Starting a business					
Getting credit					
Enforcing contracts					
Employing workers					
Paying taxes					
Dealing with licenses					
Registering property					
Protecting investors					
Trading across borders					
Closing a business					
Any other (please list)					

e) Do you have any comments about the methodology underlying the DB indicators?

f) Overall, your country is ranked A out of B by the DB 2007 report. Do you agree with this ranking? Why or Why not?

Indicator	Ranking	Indicator	Ranking	Comments
1. Starting a business		6. Registering property		
2. Employing workers		7. Dealing with licenses		
3. Getting credit		8. Trading across borders		
4. Enforcing contracts		9. Investor protection		
5. Paying taxes		10. Closing a business		

III. Use of the DB indicators

g) Have you ever used the DB indicators in the course of your work? How have you used them? Please specify. (If not, skip to Q10).

h) Please rank the use of the DB indicators specifically in:

	1. Very useful	2. Useful	3. Slightly useful	4. Not useful	Comments
Motivating reform					
Starting dialogue with country policy makers					
Creating consensus among stakeholders					
Other (please specify)....					
Designing reforms					
Suggestions on changes in legislation					
Prioritization of reform areas					
Other (please specify)....					

i) Please rank the usefulness of the following characteristics of the DBI?

	1. Very useful	2. Useful	3. Slightly useful	4. Not useful	Comments
Specific indicators? (Please list)					
Use of country benchmarking					
In-depth analysis of laws					
Media coverage of the DB indicators					
Other?					

j) What other indicators did you find to be useful when designing policy or activities for developing domestic private enterprises? In you view, what is the relative value of the DB indicators to these other indicators?

k) Please tell us about your involvement, if any, with the Bank group's Doing Business team.
- During preparation of the report?
- Commenting on the indicators?

IV. Impact of DB indicators:

l) In your view, in order of importance, what have been the major reforms that have aided or hindered the development of the domestic private enterprise in your country over the last 5 years?

m) The DB reports over the last 3 years list the following reforms in your country (see table). In your view, how significant are these reforms to the development of domestic enterprises and why?

Reforms noted by DB	1. Very significant	2. Significant	3. Slightly significant	4. Not significant	Comments

n) In your view, to what extent did the DB initiative, including DB reports, contribute to these reforms?

Thank you.

Chapter 1

1. Key articles include Djankov and others (2002), Botero and others (2004), Dollar and others (2005). See also Djankov (2008) for a more complete list.

2. See Commander and Tinn (2007), pp. 3-4. Djankov (2007) also notes "nearly all the work [on the effects of reform using ease of enterprise indicators] is cross-sectional, or uses panel analysis with an aggregate measure of economic freedom that may exaggerate the effects of reform. And researchers generally lack good microeconomic outcome indicators—like new business start-ups, number of newly registered properties, job created, increases in productivity—so much of the work makes implausible attempts to link specific regulatory reforms to overall investment, employment rate and growth" (p. 10).

3. Enterprise surveys are not available for Algeria, China, Netherlands, and Nigeria for the years 2004–07. Rwanda is not covered in the 2007/2008 Global Competitiveness Report.

4. This evaluation finds that the overall EODB ranking is highly correlated with the World Development Forum's Global Competitiveness Index (0.81) and the Economist Intelligence Unit's Business Environment Rankings (0.88), both perceptions-based indicators. Mas (2006) found similar results using the Heritage Foundation's Economic Freedom Index and IMD's World Competitiveness Scoreboard, among others. DB's 10 indicators are highly correlated with comparable subcomponents of the Global Competitiveness Index or the Business Environment Rankings only in high-income countries (around 0.70). In middle- and low-income countries, the DB indicators are weakly correlated with perception-based surveys. However, given the differences in the methodology underlying both data sets, a correlation analysis alone may not be sufficient to provide generalizable conclusions on whether or not the DB adds new information.

5. Other constraints raised by stakeholders include political and macroeconomic instability, corruption, extensive state ownership of land, and excessive oversight and regulation of private sector activities.

6. This study used the Bank's firm-level data provided by the Business Environment and Enterprise Performance Surveys (BEEPS) for 26 countries in Europe and the former Soviet Union.

7. Revenue efficiency measures how much revenue a company needs to take in to produce its net earnings. It is the ratio of net earnings and revenue.

8. Made available upon request and will be posted on the IEG Web site.

9. The DB team has produced background papers on 8 of the 10 topics; 3 are published in the *Quarterly Journal of Economics,* 2 in the *Journal of Financial Economics,* and 3 as National Bureau of Economic Research Working Papers. A complete list of these papers is available at http://www.doingbusiness.org/MethodologySurveys/

10. Except for protection of minority shareholders.

11. The seven indicators are: *starting a business, dealing with licenses, registering property, paying taxes, trading across borders, enforcing contracts,* and *closing a business.*

12. Management notes that the *starting a business* indicator rewards countries for simplifying the way that regulations are implemented, not for cutting regulation. What counts as simplification is unifying procedures or putting them on the internet so there is less hassle and fewer opportunities to extract bribes. Djankov (2008) gives the example of *starting a business* where simplifying regulations increases legal certainty.

IEG notes that DB reports and data on *starting a business* do not consistently distinguish between eliminating procedures and simplifying them through unification because they refer to some steps and procedures as being "cut," "eliminated," and "lifted."

13. The indicator measures the steps needed to get a construction permit to build a warehouse; it does not deal with licenses, permits, and authorizations in general. This point is discussed further in chapter 3.

14. Management notes that the *starting a business* indicator rewards countries for simplifying the way that regulations are implemented, not for cutting regulation. What counts as simplification is unifying procedures or putting them on the internet so there is less hassle and fewer opportunities to extract bribes. Djankov (2008) gives the example of starting a business where simplifying regulations increases legal certainty.

IEG refers to its comment in endnote 12.

15. Estimates by the evaluation team found correlations greater than 0.90 between the original rankings and others produced with alternative weighting schemes.

16. Management notes that the benefits of regulation can only be assessed in empirical analyses that link the costs that regulations incur on businesses (what DB measures) to economic and social outcomes. The background research provided by the DB team, and available at http://www.doingbusiness.org/MethodologySurveys/, does precisely that; as do numerous academic papers listed on the same Web site http://www.doingbusiness.org/documents/Citations_of_Doing_Busines_research_papers.pdf. The development of the DB indicators has made such research possible. This is illustrated in the 2006 evaluation of World Bank research and flagship publications, commissioned by then-Chief Economist and Senior Vice-President of DEC Francois Bourguignon. The report states "In fact, I believe that Doing Business is one of the most influential research initiatives that the IFC and the World Bank have ever undertaken. It has put the focus on improving the efficiency of government policy and ignited a vigorous discussion in emerging markets. This cannot only be seen by the fact that the first three entries under 'doing business' (which is even an extremely generic word combination) on Google link to the Doing Business Web site at the World Bank. Moreover, literally at any policy forum in developing countries I have heard reference to the reports." Furthermore, the Bourguignon report comments "Overall the implementation and execution of the data collection was very carefully conducted and has undergone several refinements and improvements. The Doing Business reports have created a very robust and reliable set of benchmark measures on regulation which are being used world wide by practitioners and academics alike. They have become a major source of country indicators on the regulatory environment of businesses world wide. Moreover, by engaging a cadre of first-rate academics (such as Oliver Hart, Andrei Shleifer, and others) the World Bank

team ensured that the data collection would be guided by the latest theory and empirical research in economics and finance."

Chapter 2

1. The evaluation attempted to contact all 68 informants who provided information on the evaluation's five focus indicators in the seven countries (Albania, Algeria, Burundi, Moldova, Mongolia, Nigeria, and Spain). Of these, 57 had provided a completed questionnaire, and the other 11 were supplemental informants consulted by the DB team in person, by telephone, or by e-mail to validate or clarify particular issues. The evaluation counts each of these as a separate informant. The evaluation team made at least 3 attempts to contact each of the 68 informants and succeeded in contacting and interviewing 59 percent (40 informants) by phone or by e-mail. Of the 28 informants who could not be contacted, 19 had unusable contact information or did not respond after repeated attempts, 7 had left their position, and 2 had died.

2. The evaluation chose 7 countries at random from the 175 countries covered by DB. In addition, it chose 6 countries at random from the list of countries classified by DB as "top reformers" in 2006 and 2007.

3. Management notes that the methodology chapter of each DB report states the selection criteria: the contributors need to live in the country surveyed by DB and need to practice in the topical area under review.

4. Non-PwC accountants (in Spain and Burundi) represented 1 percent.

5. In Burundi and Nigeria, Bank Group staff reported that at least one informant lacked professional expertise on the topic.

6. In *Doing Business 2007,* 17 out of 201 informants in the 13 countries reviewed did not wish to be publicly named.

7. For the five focus indicators in the seven country case study countries.

8. Four countries had only one informant. Where there were multiple informants (Mongolia, Nigeria, and Spain), the published data were not directly the median value of the responses of the questionnaires.

9. Albania, Algeria, China, Moldova, Netherlands, and Tanzania.

10. Internal correspondence on *Doing Business 2007.*

11. This figure excludes about 295 changes caused by revisions in GNI data, which affect data points ex-

pressed as a ratio with per capita GNI in the denominator.

12. Internal correspondence with DB team dated November 14, 2007.

13. This calculation excludes the changes for the *protecting investors* indicator. The nature of the indexes in this indicator makes the 10 percent rule inapplicable.

14. The World Development Indicators (WDI), for instance, make available previously published data sets through annual CD-ROMs. Management notes that this example does not support the evaluation team's claim that DB should make available all previously published data sets, uncorrected for errors and without updating them with the latest methodology. The WDI annually publishes the time-series of its data, but each publication corrects errors found in previous years. This is exactly what DB does when reporting the time-series data on its Web site: http://www.doingbusiness.org/Custom Query/.

IEG notes that it recommends that DB disclose and make available the data it has previously published but subsequently supplanted with revised or corrected data. This is the type of data provided on WDI's CD-ROMs.

15. These changes were calculated after excluding the three new countries incorporated in *Doing Business 2008*.

16. Simulations use the *Doing Business 2007* report as the baseline.

17. The standard deviation gives an estimate of the dispersion within a distribution. A normal distribution contains 65 percent of observations within one standard deviation from the mean in both directions. Greater values than 65 percent would suggest a tighter distribution skewed to one side, with few outliers on the opposite tail. The greater the number of observations within one standard deviation from the mean, the more concentrated the distribution is on one side, as seen in figure B.1 in appendix B.

18. Calculation derived using the reforms and data from *Doing Business 2007*.

Chapter 3

1. *Doing Business 2007,* p. 61: "The DB methodology....us[es] factual information about what laws and regulations say....Having representative samples of respondents is not an issue, as the texts of the relevant laws and regulations are collected and answers checked for accuracy."

2. Seventy-six percent of the 79 questions that make up the ranking in *Doing Business 2007* ask about laws and formal regulations.

3. "By law, does management remain in control of the company's assets upon the initiation of a reorganization procedure?" Question 1, section 8, legal rights index for the *getting credit* indicator. A score of 1 is assigned if management does not stay during reorganization and an administrator is responsible for managing the business during reorganization (equivalent to a response of "no" to this question).

4. *Doing Business 2007,* p. 61, acknowledges that "The measures of time involve an element of judgment by the expert respondents. When sources indicate different estimates, the time indicators reported present the median values of several responses."

5. Seven of the 10 DB indicators include a subindicator on cost that is used in the calculation of the EODB ranking. All these cost subindicators include official legal fees and, in all but one case, also include informants' estimates of costs of professional fees charged by lawyers, notaries, accountants, and the like (the exception is the firing cost for *employing workers*). For example, the cost of *enforcing contracts* subindicator includes court fees, as well as attorney fees and enforcement fees necessary for the plaintiff to enforce judgment through a public sale of the defendant's movable goods. The costs for *registering property* include the cost of registration materials, registration fees, property taxes, as well as professional fees for lawyers and notaries.

6. The *getting credit* questionnaire asks in question 2, section 11, "What in your opinion are the main areas of secured transactions law that require reform? Why?"

7. The *starting a business* questionnaire asks in question 6: "In your opinion, is the company registration process more or less efficient now in comparison to the previous year?" and in question 7: "If you were to advise the government on how to reform business start-up, what would be your main suggestion and why?"

8. Yammarino, Skinner, and Childers (1991), a meta-analysis of 115 studies on techniques to induce mail survey response rates, found survey length to have a significant effect on response rates, regardless of the target population.

9. The other legal origins are Nordic (5), German (20), and Socialist (11). The legal origin of the remain-

ing 4 countries is not available. This classification is based on *Doing Business 2004* and completed for the missing countries using the original source of the classification, the *CIA Factbook*.

10. Organization for the Harmonization of Business Law in Africa, or L'Organisation pour l'Harmonisation en Afrique du Droit des Affaires in French.

11. Based on a regression analysis of ratings on all 32 subindicators and the DB 2007 revised data, and controlling for per capita income. See appendix D.

12. On *protecting investors,* for instance, legal experts suggest that the DB's focus on allowing proxies by e-mail, use of cumulative voting, and the right of a shareholder to sue management all reflect the common law perspective.

13. Interview with external and Bank Group subject matter experts.

14. Calculation is based on the published *Doing Business 2007* data. GNI per capita data was obtained from the DB Web site for the corresponding period.

15. Excluding the poorest 35 countries in the world.

16. Countries in the top and bottom quintiles of the income per capita rank.

17. Calculations are based on *Doing Business 2007.*

18. See Djankov and others (2002). The article was largely inspired by Hernando de Soto's study of entry regulation in Peru in which the high costs of establishing a business denied economic opportunities to the poor. See de Soto (1990).

19. This framework is used neither to allocate resources nor to guide IDA programs ex-ante. See World Bank (2007b).

20. *Doing Business 2004,* p. 21, discusses some caveats on one-stop shops. These caveats are less prominent in reports of later years.

21. This paper uses the World Bank Group Entrepreneurship Survey database, which does not contain information about the sustainability of firms, an important consideration when looking at longer-term impacts.

22. Yakovlev and Zhuravskaya (2007) on Russia and Monteiro and Assuncao (2006) on Brazil.

23. Interview with PwC on October 16, 2007.

24. For the 33 countries where PwC does not operate, DB informants are local accounting firms.

25. Interview with PwC on October 16, 2007.

26. Management notes that the underlying methodology for the *paying taxes* indicator is provided by

Djankov and others (2008), NBER Working Paper 13756, which also details the differences between this methodology and a previous total tax rate methodology developed by PwC. Management also notes that in accounting and auditing services it is the standard to have a sole provider: in 2007, PwC firms provided exclusive auditing services for 368 of the companies in the Fortune 500 and 422 of the companies in the *Financial Times* Global 500. Having a single provider does not jeopardize the quality of data since the DB coding is based on the text of tax laws, which PwC provides to the DB team for verification.

IEG notes that page 29 states that "DB adopted a version of PwC's methodology in 2005" and that "the methodology is the most complex of all DB indicators because it requires detailed calculations of a variety of taxes for a standard firm."

27. Reflected in improvements in the rigidity of hours index from 60 to 20 and in the difficulty of firing index from 70 to zero. The DB staff makes adjustments in reported data from one year to the next, which are shown on its Web site. In this case, there was no such adjustment.

28. Until 2006, this indicator involved a dispute around a bounced check or a simple debt default. But since most countries have specific legislation surrounding defaults on negotiable instruments such as checks, the case study was revised for DB 2007 to entail a contractual dispute over the quality of goods.

29. The *Doing Business 2008* report made four changes: 1) The list of procedures was revised to accommodate the fact that in civil law countries the judge appoints an independent expert, while in common law countries parties send the court a list of their expert witnesses. 2) Two elements were added to the standard scenario: one on attaching the defendant's goods prior to judgment and another on providing expert opinions. 3) To reflect the overall efficiency of court procedures, one procedure is subtracted for countries that have specialized commercial courts and one procedure is subtracted for countries that allow electronic filing of court cases. 4) The cost indicator includes all fees for enforcing judgments.

30. Based on the 2005 World Bank Business Enterprise Survey for Romania.

Chapter 4

1. Interview with FIAS management.

2. *Doing Business 2008,* p. 39. The full quotation is:

"Countries that make it easier to pay taxes and contributions also have higher rates of workforce participation, and lower rates of unemployment, among women. The reason is simple: a burdensome tax system disproportionately hurts smaller businesses, especially in the services sector and this is where most women work."

3. The road shows are sponsored by the country office with minimal contributions from headquarters ($2,000 per road show).

4. In addition, since 2004, USAID has provided $211,000 to expand DB's coverage to 7 post-conflict countries. The DB also received $75,000 from the sale of reports to USAID field offices. USAID provided $1 million to finance state- and municipal-level DB exercises managed by FIAS and research on best practice reforms. Budget detail provided by Knowledge Management and Outreach Team in the Office of the Vice President, FPD, World Bank-IFC in an e-mail dated November 27, 2007.

5. From the case studies for a forthcoming IEG evaluation of the Bank's economic and sector work (ESW).

6. The section is based on 100 interviews with Bank Group staff and stakeholders in all the case study countries, plus reports from interviews in other countries held by a forthcoming evaluation reviewing Bank ESW, and interviews with international donor agencies including MCC and USAID.

7. Respondents rated usefulness on a four-point scale: very useful, useful, slightly useful, or not useful. Thirteen percent of Bank Group staff and stakeholders considered the use of country benchmarking to be either "not useful" or "slightly useful," either because they felt the data and/or ranking for their country were inaccurate, or because they believed cross-country comparisons were inappropriate because it obscured the importance of country context.

8. Bank management comments on *Doing Business 2008* report.

9. Interviews with FIAS Rapid Response Unit and MCC staff.

10. Interview with management of the FIAS Rapid Response Unit.

11. Management notes that all data used in background research by the DB team are available at http://www.doingbusiness.org/MethodologySurveys/; if a researcher wishes to replicate the work by another academic who used previous versions of DB data, the latter is obliged to provide these data on request upon publication of her research. The IEG recommendation to make available uncorrected data and data unadjusted for the latest methodology is unorthodox: this is not practiced by major data providers.

IEG notes that the evaluation's recommendation refers to data published periodically by DB (on its Web site and in publications) that are subsequently removed and supplanted by revised or corrected data. DB does not currently make these data available.

12. The exact formula is: IDA country allocation per annum = base allocation $+ f$ (Country performance rating 2.0, Population 1.0, GNI/capita-0.125) where CPIA accounts for 80 percent of the country performance rating. See World Bank (2007c).

13. See Approach Paper for IEG's Special Study on the Bank's CPIA, February 5, 2008.

14. Only operations approved between fiscal years 2004 and 2007 are included. The six countries are: Albania, Moldova, Nigeria, Peru, Rwanda, and Tanzania.

15. Mentioned in Burundi, Moldova, Nigeria, Netherlands, Peru, Rwanda, and Tanzania.

Appendix A

1. Serbia & Montenegro was removed from the random selection process because the country split in 2006. Georgia and Romania were top reformers in both years, but were included only once in the random selection process.

Appendix B

1. The data used in this appendix corresponds to *Doing Business 2007*.

2. The simulation uses the indicator value in *Doing Business 2008* (after a reform) and measures the impact of the reform on indicator rankings and the EODB ranking for 2007, holding other countries' actions constant.

3. The standard deviation can give a good estimate of the dispersion within a distribution. A normal distribution contains 65 percent of observations within one standard deviation from the mean in both directions. Greater values than 65 percent could suggest a tighter distribution skewed to one side, with a few outliers on the opposite tail: the greater the number of observations within one standard deviation from the mean, the more concentrated the distribution.

4. Five of the 32 subindicators, 4 of which are in *trading across borders,* have been excluded because it is difficult to assign specific reforms to them.

Appendix D

1. The data used in this appendix correspond to the updated version for DB 2007, downloaded from the DB Web site in October 2007.

2. The basis for this classification can be found on page 115 of *Doing Business 2004*. This database has information for 130 countries. Information for the additional 45 countries was retrieved from the source used by *Doing Business 2004*—the *CIA Factbook*. The category "common law" used in this report corresponds directly to the category "English" in *Doing Business 2004*, and the category "civil law" corresponds to the category "French."

3. This variable includes cash receipts from taxes, social contributions, and other revenues such as fines, fees, rent, and income from property or sales.

4. A good variable to add to this analysis would have been public contributions to social welfare programs as a share of GDP. However, such a variable is available for a limited amount of countries, which made it impractical to use.

Acemoglu, Daron, and Simon Johnson. 2005. "Unbundling Institutions." *Journal of Political Economy* 113(5): 949–95.

Altenburg, Tilman, and C. von Drachenfels. 2006. "The 'New Minimalist Approach' to Private Sector Development: A Critical Assessment." *Development Policy Review* 24 (4): 387–411.

Arruñada, Benito. 2007. "Pitfalls to Avoid When Measuring Institutions: Is 'Doing Business' Damaging Business?" Universitat Pompeu Fabra Economics and Business Working Paper No. 1040, August 24. http://www.econ.upf.edu/docs/papers/downloads/1040.pdf

Arvis, Jean-Francois, Monica Alina Mustra, John Panzer, Lauri Ojala, and Tapio Naula. 2007. *Connecting to Compete: Trade Logistics in the Global Economy.* Washington, DC: World Bank.

Ayyagari, Meghana, Asli Demirguc-Kunt, and Vojislav Aksimovic. 2005. "How Important Are Financing Constraints? The Role of Finance in the Business Environment." World Bank Policy Research Working Paper No. 3820. World Bank, Washington, DC.

Bakvis, Peter. 2006. "How the World Bank and IMF Use the Doing Business Report to Promote Labour Market Deregulation in Developing Countries." Prepared for the International Confederation of Free Trade Unions, Washington, DC. http://www.gurn.info/topic/prsp/doingbusiness.pdf

Beck, Thorsten, and Asli Demirguc-Kunt. 2006. "Small and Medium-Size Enterprises: Access to Finance as a Growth Constraint." *Journal of Banking & Finance* 30: 2931–43.

Beck, Thorsten, Asli Demirguc-Kunt, and Ross Levine. 2003. "Law and Firms' Access to Finance." NBER Working Paper 10687. National Bureau of Economic Research, Cambridge, MA.

Beck, Thorsten, Asli Demirgu-Kunt, Luc Laeven, and Vojislav Maksimovic. 2003. "The Determinants of Financing Obstacles." World Bank Policy Research Working Paper No. 3204. World Bank, Washington, DC.

Berg, Janine, and Sandrine Cazes. 2007. "The Doing Business Indicators: Measurement Issues and Political Implications." Economic and Labour Market Paper No. 2007/6. Geneva: International Labor Organization. http://www.ilo.org/public/english/employment/download/elm/elm07-6.pdf

Biggs, Tyler. 2004. "The Investment Climate and Private Sector Development." Background Paper prepared for *Improving Investment Climates: An Evaluation of World Bank Group Assistance.* IEG–World Bank, Washington, DC.

Blanchet, Didier. 2006. "Exploratory Analysis of the Indicators Proposed by Doing Business Reports 2005 and 2006 of the World Bank." Attractivité Economique du Droit Working Paper No. AED-EAL-2006-3. Paris.

Botero, Juan, Simeon Djankov, Rafael Porta, and Florencio Lopez-De-Silanes. 2004. "The Regulation of Labor." *The Quarterly Journal of Economics* 119(4): 1339–82.

Bruhn, Miriam. 2007. "License to Sell: The Effect of Business Registration Reform on Entrepreneurial Activity in Mexico." MIT Job Market Paper (2007); World Bank Policy Research Working Paper (2008). http://siteresources.worldbank.org/DEC/Resources/BruhnOct2007.pdf

Carlin, Wendy, and Paul Seabright. 2007. "Bring Me Sunshine: Which Part of the Business Climate Should Public Policy Try to Fix?" Paper presented at the Annual Bank Conference on Development Economics, May, Bled, Slovenia. http://siteresources.worldbank.org/INTABCDESLO2007/Resources/SeabrightCarlinPaper.pdf

Commander, Simon, and Jan Svejnar. 2007. "Do Institutions, Ownership, Exporting and Competition Explain Firm Performance? Evidence from 26 Transition Countries." IZA Working Paper 2637. Institute for the Study of Labor, Bonn, Germany.

Commander, Simon, and Katrin Tinn. 2007. "Evaluating Doing Business." Background paper prepared for this evaluation. Available at: www.worldbank.org/ieg

Cunat, Alejandro, and Marc Melitz. 2007. "Volatility, Labor Market Flexibility, and the Pattern of Comparative Advantage." NBER Working Paper 13062. National Bureau of Economic Research, Cambridge, MA.

Davis, Kevin E., and Michael B. Kruse. 2007. "Taking the Measure of Law: The Case of the Doing Business Project." *Law & Social Inquiry* 32(4): 1095–119.

De Sa, Lilliana. 2005. "Business Registration Start-up: A Concept Note." IFC Working Paper. International Finance Corporation, Washington, DC. http://www.ifc .org/ifcext/sme.nsf/AttachmentsByTitle/BEEBus RegStartup.pdf/$FILE/BEEBusRegStartup.pdf

de Soto, Hernando. 1990. *The Other Path*. New York, NY: Harper and Row.

Djankov, Simeon. 2008. "A Response to *Is Doing Business Damaging Business*." http://www.doingbus iness.org/documents/Response_to_Arrunada_JCE.pdf (forthcoming, *Journal of Comparative Economics*)

———. 2007. "Measuring the Ease of Enterprise." http://www.doingbusiness.org/documents/ Measur-ing_the_Ease_of_Enterprise.pdf

Djankov, Simeon, Caroline Freund, and Cong Pham. 2007. "Trading on Time." http://www.doingbus iness.org/documents/trading_on_time_full_report.pdf

Djankov, Simeon, Caralee McLiesh, and Andrei Shleifer. 2007. "Private Credit in 129 Countries." *Journal of Financial Economics* 84(2): 299–329.

Djankov, Simeon, Oliver Hart, Caralee McLiesh, and Andrei Shleifer. 2006. "Debt Enforcement around the World." NBER Working Paper 12807. National Bureau of Economic Research, Cambridge, MA.

Djankov, Simeon, Rafael La Porta, Florencio Lopez-De-Silanes, and Andrei Shleifer. 2007. "The Law and Economics of Self-Dealing." http://www.doingbusi ness.org/documents/Protecting-Investors-Self-Dealing.pdf (forthcoming, *Journal of Financial Economics*)

Djankov, Simeon, Caralee McLiesh, Rita Ramalho, and Andrei Shleifer. 2008. "The Effect of Corporate Taxes on Investment and Entrepreneurship." NBER Work-ing Paper 13756. National Bureau of Economic Re-search, Cambridge, MA. http://www.nber.org/papers/ w13756

Djankov, Simeon, Rafael La Porta, Florencio Lopez-De-Silanes, and Andrei Shleifer. 2003. "Courts." *The Quarterly Journal of Economics* 118(2): 453–517.

———. 2002. "The Regulation of Entry." *The Quar-terly Journal of Economics* 117(1): 1–37.

Dollar, David, Mary Hallward-Dreimeier, and Taye Mengistae. 2005. "Investment Climate and Firm Per-formance in Developing Economies." *Economic De-velopment and Cultural Change* 54 (1): 1–31.

Dorbec, Anna. 2006. "Credit Information Systems: The-oretical and Comparative Analysis." Working Paper AED-EAL-2006-2. Attractivité Economique du Droit (AED), University of Paris X-Nanterre.

Du Marais, Bertrand. 2006. "Methodological Limits of the 'Doing Business' Reports." Working Paper AED-2006-1. Attractivité Economique du Droit, University of Paris X-Nanterre.

Eiffert, Benn. 2007. "The Economic Response to Regu-latory Reform, 2003–06." Paper commissioned for the Center for Global Development. http://beifert .googlepages.com/eifertinvestmentresponseto reform10-2.doc

Freeman, Richard B. 2007. "Labor Market Institutions around the World." NBER Working Paper 13242. Na-tional Bureau of Economic Research, Cambridge, MA.

Galiani, S., and E. Schargrodsky. 2005. "Property Rights for the Poor: Effects of Land Titling." Universidad Tor-cuato Di Tella, Centro de Investigación en Finanzas, Business School Working Paper Series, Buenes Aires.

Hall, Robert E., and Charles I. Jones. 1999. "Why Do Some Countries Produce So Much More Output per Worker Than Others?" *The Quarterly Journal of Economics* 114(1):83–116.

Hammergren, Linn. 2002. "Performance Indicators for Judicial Reform Projects." World Bank. http://site re-sources.worldbank.org/INTLAWJUSTINST/ Resources/Hammergrenperformance.pdf

Hausmann, Ricardo, Dani Rodrik, and Andrés Velasco. 2005. "Growth Diagnostics." John F. Kennedy School of Government, Harvard University, Cambridge, MA. http://ksghome.harvard.edu/~drodrik/ barcelona finalmarch2005.pdf

Hellmann, Joel, and Mark Schankerman. 2000. "Inter-vention, Corruption and Capture: The Nexus be-tween Enterprises and the State." *Economics of Transition* 8(3): 545–76.

Heritage Foundation. 2007. *2007 Index of Economic Freedom*. Washington, DC: Heritage Foundation.

IMF (International Monetary Fund). 2007. *Revised Guide on Resource Revenue Transparency*. Fiscal Affairs Department. Washington, DC: IMF.

Jappelli, Tullio, and Marco Pagano. 2002. "Information Sharing, Lending and Defaults: Cross-country Evidence." *Journal of Banking & Finance* 26: 2017–45.

Kaplan, David S., Enrique Seira, and Eduardo Piedra. 2007. "Entry Regulation and Business Start-Ups: Evidence from Mexico." World Bank Policy Research Working Paper 4322. World Bank, Washington, DC.

Kauffmann, Daniel. 2002. "Governance Crossroads." In *Global Competitiveness Report, 2002–2003,* ed. Peter K. Cornelius. New York: Oxford University Press for the World Economic Forum.

Kaufmann, D., A. Kraay, and M. Mastruzzi. 2006. "Governance Matters V: Governance Indicators for 1996–2005." World Bank Policy Research Working Paper 4012. World Bank, Washington, DC.

Kaufmann, D., A. Kraay, and P. Ziodo-Lobaton. 1999. "Governance Matters." World Bank Policy Research Working Paper 2196. World Bank, Washington, DC.

Kenyon, Thomas. 2007. "How to Encourage Enterprise Formalization: Some Practical Hints for Policymakers in Africa." *FIAS Policy Note.* http://www.fias.net/ifcext/fias.nsf/AttachmentsByTitle/June2007Policy NoteEnterpriseFormalization/$FILE/FIAS+Enterprise+Formalization+in+Africa.pdf

Klapper, Leora, Luc Laeven, and Raghuram Rajan. 2006. "Entry Regulation as a Barrier to Entrepreneurship." *Journal of Financial Economics* 82(3): 591–629.

Klapper, Leora, Raphael Amit, Mauro F. Guillen, and Juan Manuel Quesada. 2007. "Entrepreneurship and Firm Formation across Countries." World Bank Policy Research Working Paper 4313. The World Bank Group, Development Research Group, Finance and Private Sector Team, Washington, DC. http://www-wds.worldbank.org/external/default/WDSContent Server/IW3P/IB/2007/10/05/000158349_200710051553 44/Rendered/PDF/wps4313.pdf

Knack, Stephen, and Phillip Keefer. 1995. "Institutions and Economic Performance: Cross-Country Tests Using Alternative Institutional Measures." *Economics and Politics* 7(3): 207–27.

La Porta, Rafael, Florencio Lopez-de-Silanes, and Andrei Shleifer. 2007. "The Economic Consequences of Legal Origins." http://www.economics.harvard.edu/faculty/shleifer/files/jel.nov_combine.pdf.pdf (forthcoming, *Journal of Economic Literature*)

Lazarus, Suellen. 2007. Statement prepared for the House Committee on Finance Services hearing on "The Fight against Global Poverty and Inequality: The World Bank's Approach to the Core Labor Standards and Employment Creation." October 3. http://www.house.gov/apps/list/hearing/finan cialsvsdem/lazarus.pdf

Love, Inessa, and Nataliya Mylenko. 2003. "Credit Reporting and Financing Constraints." World Bank Policy Research Working Paper 3142. World Bank, Washington, DC.

Loayza, Norman V., Ana Maria Oviedo, and Luis Serven. 2004. "Regulation and Macroeconomic Performance." World Bank Policy Research Working Paper 3469. World Bank, Washington, DC.

Maldives government, Ministry of Planning and National Development. 2007. "Seventh National Development Plan 2006–2010—Creating New Opportunities." http://www.planning.gov.mv/en/images/stories/wdp/seventh-ndp.pdf

Mas, Ignacio. 2006. *A Comparison of the World Bank/IFC's Doing Business Regulatory Indicators with Other Business Environment Indicators.* Final Report prepared for the Financial and Private Sector Vice Presidency of the World Bank Group. May 31.

Messick, Richard E. 2005. "What Governments Can Do to Facilitate the Enforcement of Contracts." Prepared for Reforming the Business Environment: From Assessing Problems to Measuring Results, Cairo, November 28–December 1. http://site resources.worldbank.org/EXTGDLNREGION ECA/Resources/872782-1163537217246/april_24b.pdf

———. 1999. "Judicial Reform and Economic Development: A Survey of the Issues." *The World Bank Observer* 14 (1): 117–36.

Monteiro, Joana, and Juliano Assunção. 2006. "Outgoing the Shadows: Estimating the Impact of Bureaucratic Simplification and Tax Cuts on Informality and Investment." Pontifica Universidade Catolica, Department of Economics, Rio de Janeiro.http:// pro fessores.ibmecrj.br/erg/wkshops/papers/2006 0331.pdf

Morris, Felipe, Victor Endo, and Rafael Ugaz. 2004. *Develando el Ministerio: La Formalization de la propiedad en el Peru.* Lima: COFOPRI-Banco Mundial.

OECD (Organisation for Economic Co-operation and Development). 2007a. "Two Broad Approaches for Tax Reform." Chapter 4 in *Economic Survey of New Zealand 2007.* Paris.http://www.oecd.org/dataoecd/39/62/38440934.pdf

—————. 2007b. "Toward a More Efficient Taxation System in New Zealand." OECD Economics Department Working Paper 557. Paris.

Polaski, Sandra. 2007. "The World Bank's Approach to Core Labor Standards and Employment Creation: Recent Developments." Testimony submitted to The United States House of Representatives Committee on Financial Services. Washington, DC. October 3. http://www.carnegieendowment.org/files/polaski-testimony.pdf

PwC (PricewaterhouseCoopers). 2007. *Paying Taxes 2008: The Global Picture.* www.pwc.com

Rodrik, Dani. 2004. "Getting Institutions Right." CESifo DICE Report, Harvard University, Cambridge, MA. http://ksghome.harvard.edu/~drodrik/ifo-institutions%20article%20_April%202004_.pdf

Sader, Frank. 2002. "Do One Stop Shops Work?" FIAS Research Working Paper, Foreign Investment Advisory Service, Washington, DC. http://www.ifc.org/ifcext/fias.nsf/AttachmentsByTitle/doonestopshopswork/$FILE/Do+One+Stop+Shops+Work.pdf

Schneider, Friedrich, and Robert Klinglmair. 2004. "Shadow Economies around the World: What Do We Know?" Center for Economic Studies & Institute for Economic Research (CESifo) Working Paper 1167. Munich. http://ssrn.com/abstract=518526

Vanuatu government. 2007. "Information about the Government of Vanuatu." Web site: http://www.vanuatugovernment.gov.vu/vanuatugov.html and accessed on December 19, 2007.

Webb, Richard, Diether Beuermann, and Carla Revilla. 2006. "La Construccion del Derecho de Propiedad – El caso de los asentamientos humanos en el Perú." Tarea Association Gráfica Educativa, Lima, Peru.

World Bank. 2007a. *Finance for All Policies and Pitfalls in Expanding Access.* Washington, DC: World Bank.

—————. 2007b. Focus on Results: The IDA14 Results Measurement System and Directions for IDA15. International Development Association–Operations Policy and Country Services. http://siteresources.worldbank.org/IDA/Resources/Seminar%20PDFs/73449-1172525976405/3492866-1175095887430/IDA15Results.pdf

—————. 2007c. "IDA's Performance-Based Allocation System: Simplification of the Formula and Other Outstanding Issues." International Development Association–Operations Policy and Country Services. http://siteresources.worldbank.org/IDA/Resources/Seminar%20PDFs/73449-1172525976405/3492866-1175095887430/PBA_Sept.2007.pdf

—————. 2007d. "The Cost of State Regulation of the Enterprise Activity." Chisinau. World Bank, Washington, DC. http://siteresources.worldbank.org/INTMOLDOVA/Resources/CoDB-2007_En.pdf

—————. 2006. "Country Policy and Institutional Assessments: 2006 Assessment Questionnaire." International Development Association, Operations Policy and Country Services, Washington, DC. http://siteresources.worldbank.org/IDA/Resources/73153-1181752621336/CPIA06CriteriaA2.pdf

—————. 2004. *World Development Report 2005: A Better Investment Climate for Everyone.* New York: World Bank and Oxford University Press.

World Bank-IFC. 2007a. "List of Academic Citations of the Doing Business Background Papers." Prepared by the Doing Business Unit. http://www.doingbusiness.org/documents/Citations_of_Doing_Business_research_papers.pdf

—————. 2007b. *Doing Business 2008.* Prepared by the Doing Business Unit. Washington, DC: World Bank.

—————. 2006a. *Reforming Business Registration Regulatory Procedures at the National Level: A Reform Toolkit for Project Teams.* Small and Medium Enterprise Department. Washington, DC: World Bank. http://www.ifc.org/ifcext/sme.nsf/AttachmentsByTitle/BEEReformBusRegNational/$FILE/Bus+Reg+Book.pdf

—————. 2006b. *Doing Business 2007.* Prepared by the Doing Business Unit. Washington, DC: World Bank.

—————. 2005a. *Doing Business 2006.* Prepared by the Doing Business Unit. Washington, DC: World Bank.

—————. 2005b. *Doing Business 2005.* Prepared by the Doing Business Unit. Washington, DC: World Bank.

—————. 2004. *Doing Business 2004.* Prepared by the Doing Business Unit. Washington, DC: World Bank.

World Economic Forum. 2007. *Global Competitiveness Report.* New York: Palgrave Macmillan.

Yammarino, Francis, Steven Skinner, and Terry Childers. 1991. "Understanding mail Survey Response Behavior." *The Public Opinion Quarterly* 55(4): 613–39.

Yakovlev, Evgeny, and Ekaterina V. Zhuravskaya. 2007. "Deregulation of Business." CEPR Discussion Paper 6610. CEPR, London. http://ssrn.com/abstract=965838

This bibliography excludes Bank Group and external documents—such as Country Assistance Strategies and donor reports—reviewed as background for each of the thirteen case study countries.